Geography Projects

Written by David Flint

Published by Scholastic Publications Ltd,
Villiers House, Clarendon Avenue,
Leamington Spa, Warwickshire CV32 5PR

© 1994 Scholastic Publications Ltd

Written by David Flint
Edited by Jane Wright
Sub-edited by Kate Banham
Illustrated by Darin Mount (Graham-
Cameron Illustration)
Designed by Micky Pledge
Front and back covers designed by
Sue Limb
Cover artwork by Mary Lack
Photograph by Martyn Chillmaid
Artwork by Liz Preece, Castle Graphics
Kenilworth
Typeset by Typesetters (Birmingham) Ltd
Printed in Great Britain by Clays Ltd

**British Library Cataloguing in Publication
Data**
A catalogue record for this book is available from the
British Library.

ISBN 0-590-53097-6

The right of David Flint to be identified as
the Author of this work has been asserted
by him in accordance with the Copyright,
Designs and Patents Act 1988.

Contents

Introduction

The purpose of this book is to provide materials which will help teachers develop the ideas, skills and knowledge of the Geography National Curriculum. Within the statutory orders, Geography is divided into five attainment targets: skills; environmental geography; knowledge and understanding of places; physical geography; human geography. Whilst it is useful to refer to the statements of attainment within each attainment target, this book suggests that the attainment targets should be combined within a series of themes. The webs provided at the beginning of each chapter show how that particular area of geographical study will draw upon and combine elements from several attainment targets. It is useful to think of geography in relation to:

1. skills (mapwork and fieldwork);
2. places (local and regional within the UK and distant places);
3. themes (physical, human and environmental).

In this way children will gain a balanced view of the people, places and environments which make up the subject.

Similarly, geography is rarely taught in isolation. Much of the content has close links with other curriculum areas, especially science and technology. Most geographical projects provide opportunities for cross-curricular work. It is for this reason that the web diagrams are included at the beginning of each chapter in the book. It is not intended that teachers pursue every curriculum area in their study; rather the webs suggest a range of possible links from which teachers can select those most appropriate to the needs of their pupils.

Some teachers have found it difficult to translate the National Curriculum statutory orders into good classroom practice. The aim of this book is to suggest ways in which this process can be achieved, so that the best elements of good primary practice are retained within the overall framework of statutory requirements. Teaching and learning in geography should be fun, and full of practical investigations focused on the world around the children.

Rocks and soil

While rocks and soil are basic to every child's environment, they are often neglected as areas of study. There is a common fallacy that only people with a background in geology and geography can successfully plan and implement work based on rocks and soil. In fact the key element of any such work is that of the enquiry process, whereby children are encouraged to ask questions about soil and rocks. These questions can then be investigated by the whole class including the teacher. It is the process of investigation which is important rather than a specific ability to identify different types of rock or soil. Although soil and rocks can be investigated all year round, the summer and early autumn terms are probably the best from the point of view of carrying out fieldwork visits.

Work on soil and rocks has clear overlaps with science. Thus, another good reason for focusing on the projects in this chapter is that statements of attainment in both Geography and Science can be met at the same time. The nature of these projects is such that they can be extended throughout the school, becoming progressively more varied as children get older.

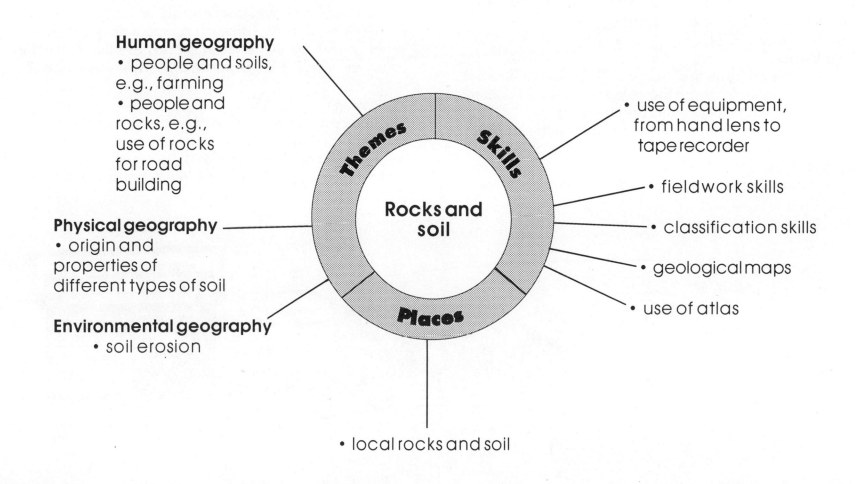

Human geography
• people and soils, e.g., farming
• people and rocks, e.g., use of rocks for road building

Physical geography
• origin and properties of different types of soil

Environmental geography
• soil erosion

Themes

Skills

Places

Rocks and soil

• use of equipment, from hand lens to tape recorder

• fieldwork skills

• classification skills

• geological maps

• use of atlas

• local rocks and soil

Studying our soil

Age range
Five to seven.

Group size
Various.

What you need
Some local soil, newspaper, a magnifying glass, dishes for earthworms or other soil animals, a tape recorder, an audio cassette, rubber or plastic gloves.

What to do
Explain to the children that they will be trying to find out as much as possible about the colour, smell and content of soil, from pebbles to plants and animals.

Open the newspaper on the floor and tip the soil sample on to it. The children (wearing the protective gloves) can spread out the soil and break up any lumps. They should be encouraged to look very closely at the soil and then describe and record (on tape) what they can see, smell and feel. Is the soil all the same colour or are some parts darker than others? Does the soil have a smell? If so, what is it like? Are the particles that make up the soil all the same size? Are there any stones or pebbles? Do they have sharp or rounded edges? Are there any live animals in the soil? If so, they should carefully pick them out and put them in containers for study before returning them to their natural habitat. What do the animals look like? How big are they? What colour are they? How do they move around?

The children should concentrate on any pieces of plant material in the soil such as roots or dead leaves. What colour are they? What shapes are they? Are they found all over the soil sample or only in some parts?

Follow-up
This process can be repeated with soil samples from different locations and of different types: a sandy soil, a peat soil, a clay soil. If in doubt, teachers can use builders' sand, peat and clay in the experiments.

Sorting rocks

Age range
Five to seven.

Group size
Pairs.

What you need
A collection of pieces of rock and stones which vary in size, colour and shape, a magnifying glass, a binocular microscope, plastic gloves.

What to do
Set out a collection of different rocks and stones on a table. Aim for a range of different colours, textures and surfaces in the rocks and stones. The children should examine each rock carefully. The first part of the task is for the children to study each rock in as much detail as possible, using the magnifying glass and, if possible, a binocular microscope. What are the colours in each rock? How many colours can you find? What is the texture of each rock?

The second part of the task is to sort the rocks and stones into groups. Let the children choose the basis for the classification. These bases may be size, colour, shape, weight, texture or a range of other criteria. Each pair should then describe the basis for their grouping to the rest of the class.

Follow-up
Additional activities to study the relative weights of the rocks and their relative hardness (can it be scratched with a finger nail or a paper clip?) can be used as the basis for additional groupings.

Settling soil

Age range
Five to eleven.

Group size
Whole class.

What you need
Three large transparent jars (glass or plastic) with lids, water, a magnifying glass, three samples of different types of soil (one sandy, one peaty, one gritty). If in doubt, take a garden soil and mix it with sand, peat and coarse grit to produce the three types of soil.

What to do
Put a sample of soil in each jar. Put the same amount in each jar until they are half full. Fill each jar with water and put on the lids.

Shake the jars then stand them on a shelf to watch the particles settle. Children should observe and record the changes as the soil particles settle out. Which particles settle out first? Which stay floating in the water? Which water clears first? How many different layers can be seen in each jar? Ask the children to draw the different layers in each jar as the particles settle out. Older children can write explanations of why the largest particles separate out first and the finest last.

Follow-up
Carry out the same experiment with soil samples from the school grounds. Try using a sample of sand and one of peat for comparison with the local soils.

Rocks, soil, water

Age range
Seven to nine.

Group size
Various.

What you need
Empty cardboard boxes, old margarine tubs, a sample of soil, a sample of rock, some water, plastic gloves.

What to do
Set up three 'feely' boxes. In one put a margarine tub filled with the sample of soil. In the second put a margarine tub filled with the sample of rock and in the third put a margarine tub filled with water. Ask the children to take turns to feel inside each box and to describe what they discover. The children should be encouraged to describe what they find in as much detail as possible. Is it hard or soft; smooth or rough; wet or dry; hot or cold; sharp or rounded; solid or liquid? The aim is to discover and describe the characteristics of rocks, soil and water which are the basic elements of the environment. Ask the children to write down a few words describing each tub of rocks, soil and water.

Follow-up
Put different types of rock and soil in the feely boxes and repeat the procedure. How do these differ from the earlier samples? In what ways are they the same?

Soil texture

Age range
Seven to nine.

Group size
Groups of three or four.

What you need
A sample of local soil, a newspaper, empty containers for soil animals, a wide mesh sieve, a fine mesh sieve, a magnifying glass, plastic bags, a weighing machine, plastic gloves.

What to do
Explain to the children that they are going to investigate the different types of soil to be found in one sample, that is, coarse, medium and fine.

Tell the children to weigh the soil sample and record the result. Next, they should open the newspaper on the floor and spread the soil sample over it. Instruct them to break up any lumps. They should then study the soil using a magnifying glass. Tell them to pick out any live animals and put these in containers. Are there any dead animals?

The children should tip all the soil into a wide mesh sieve and shake it through on to another sheet of newspaper. Stones, pebbles and large particles will be left in the sieve. Explain that this is the coarse part of the soil. They should weigh it and record the results.

Now tell them to put the soil on the newspaper through a fine mesh sieve on to another piece of newspaper. The soil which remains in the sieve is the medium soil. Again this should be weighed and the results recorded. Finally, they should weigh the fine soil which has passed through the fine mesh sieve, and record the results. Now ask the children to draw a bar graph to show the amounts of fine, medium and coarse soil in their sample.

Follow-up
The process could be repeated using soil from different locations around the school. How do they vary in terms of the percentage of coarse, medium and fine soil? What does this say about the soil in the school grounds? What conclusions can be drawn about soil types in school?

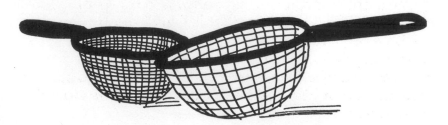

The dirty hands test

Age range
Seven to eleven.

Group size
Pairs.

What you need
Three or four samples of different types of soil (e.g., peat, sand and clay); a small amount of water, photocopiable page 117.

What to do
Let each pair take one soil sample. Then tell them to follow the procedure on photocopiable page 117 in order to find out which type of soil they are studying. The procedure is called the dirty hands test (for obvious reasons!).

As they carry out the sequence of activities shown on photocopiable page 117 ask the children to record their results. At the end they should be able to identify their soil type. Then tell them to repeat the dirty hands test on another sample and reach a conclusion as to its type.

Follow-up
This experiment can be repeated with a range of samples of different types of soil. Children will soon become proficient at carrying out the test and thus at identifying the soil type. The test can be used on different sections of the same soil, for example a sample from the top of a soil and one from the bottom. How do they compare?

A soil profile

Age range
Seven to eleven.

Group size
Whole class.

What you need
A spade, a one metre length of wood, liquid adhesive, a spatula, a ruler, a newspaper, a magnifying glass, plastic gloves.

What to do
Choose an area of ground away from trees and hedges. Get the children to take it in turns to dig a hole about half a metre square and a metre deep.

Ask them to study the soil which has been exposed by the digging. Can they see different layers in the soil from the top downwards? Tell them to look for plant roots in the top part of the soil and to measure how far down the plant roots go. Wearing the plastic gloves, ask the children to take a small sample of soil from this top layer, put it on a newspaper and examine it carefully with a magnifying glass. What plant and animal remains can they find? They should repeat this for each of the other layers they can see in the soil.

Tell the children to measure the depth of the other layers of the soil, and to mark these depths on the strip of wood. They should then spread adhesive over one side of the strip of wood, and sprinkle a small amount of soil from the top layer on the top part of the strip of wood. This should be repeated for each of the layers in the soil. When complete they have created a record of how the soil changes with depth. This record is called a soil monolith.

Follow-up
Children can make soil monoliths of the profiles in other places, for example near hill tops and in valleys, or in gardens or on heaths. In each case be sure they return the soil to the hole and cause no damage to the site.

Making a fossil

Age range
Seven to eleven.

Group size
Groups of four.

What you need
A collection of fossils (plants and animals), a bowl, a plastic tub, petroleum jelly, a sea shell, plaster of Paris, a spoon, plastic gloves.

What to do
Fossils come in two main types – an imprint fossil or an actual fossil. An imprint is the shape the fossil makes in the surrounding rock. It will show the shape, size and pattern of the fossil in the same way as a footprint shows the shape, size and pattern of the sole of a shoe.

An actual fossil is a plant or animal whose tissue has been completely replaced by rock. The shape, size and features can be clearly seen but the fossil is made of solid rock.

Tell the children to study the collection of fossil plants and animals and then to sort them into two groups, one of actual fossils and one of the imprints of fossils.

Explain to the children that they are going to make their own fossils. First, they should half fill the bowl with water then stir in plaster of Paris until it is like a thick cream. Then they should pour the plaster into the tub and cover the sea shell with petroleum jelly. When the plaster is starting to harden they should press the shell into the plaster without submerging it. When the plaster sets they should have an imprint fossil of their shell.

Next, the children should smear petroleum jelly on to the imprint fossil in the tub. Some more plaster of Paris should be made up and this poured into the fossil imprint. When the plaster has set, the plaster fossil can be lifted out of its mould. Assemble each group's fossils and make a class display as part of a project on fossils.

Follow-up
The children could repeat the experiment using different sizes and shapes of shells. They could also use real fossils to create the imprints, but care needs to be taken in covering them completely in petroleum jelly to prevent damage by the plaster.

CLASS 3B-FOSSIL PROJECT

Splash pillars

Age range
Seven to eleven.

Group size
Pairs.

What you need
Each group needs light coloured blotting paper, an empty litre milk carton, some pebbles, elastic bands, a compass.

What to do
Explain that the aim of the activity is to make a series of splash pillars which will be used to test how raindrops can cause soil to be washed away.

Tell each pair to fold the blotting paper around the carton so that all four sides are covered, and use the elastic bands to hold it in place. They should place some stones in the bottom of the carton to anchor it, then mark North, South, East and West at the top of each side of the splash pillar.

Explain how raindrops splash upwards when they hit the ground surface. This splash can carry away soil. The splash varies with the intensity of the rain, the type of ground surface and the location of the surface.

During a rainstorm help the children to put their splash pillars outdoors around the school on different surfaces such as tarmac, grass and bare soil. Tell them to use a compass to position each pillar with the correct side facing north. They should also try to situate splash pillars around school in a variety of places such as in the open, close to a hedge, close to buildings and facing into the wind.

Let the children leave their pillars for about five minutes then get them to bring them indoors to examine the splash marks. Some key questions for the children to investigate are:
- On which splash pillar is there soil? (Usually from bare soil.)
- On which side of the pillar were the highest splash marks?
- Which splash pillar (on tarmac, grass, bare soil) had the highest splash marks? (Usually tarmac.)
- Which place had most splash erosion? (Bare soil.)
- Which had least? (Grass and tarmac.)
- Ask the children to identify what factors influenced the amount and height of the splash (wind speed, wind direction, rainfall intensity, aspect, ground surface).

Follow-up
Tell the children to locate splash pillars under trees and bushes or next to fences and compare results. They could also use splash pillars in the same places during a light shower and in a heavy downpour and compare results.

Absorbing water

Age range
Seven to eleven.

Group size
Pairs.

What you need
Six soft drink cans (same size), five of which should have the top and bottom removed and a mark made 1cm from the rim on each, a measuring cylinder, a stop-watch.

What to do
Explain that the purpose of the activity is to see how quickly soils can absorb water. This rate of absorption can vary with a range of factors such as soil type and the degree to which the soil has been trampled.

Tell the children to press five of the cans 1cm into samples of each of the following types of soil – a clay soil, a sand pit, a rich garden soil, a lawn, an area of grass which has been heavily trampled. Let them use the measuring cylinder to pour the same amount of water into each can. The children should time how long it takes for all the water to soak into the soil. They should stop timing when no more water remains in the can (there may be a long wait with some samples).

For each can, the children should record its location, the soil type and the time required for the water to soak away. They should note in which soils water soaks away fastest and in which soils water soaks away very slowly.

Follow-up
Ask the children to time absorption rates at different sites around the school field. Which places are free-draining? Which need better drainage?

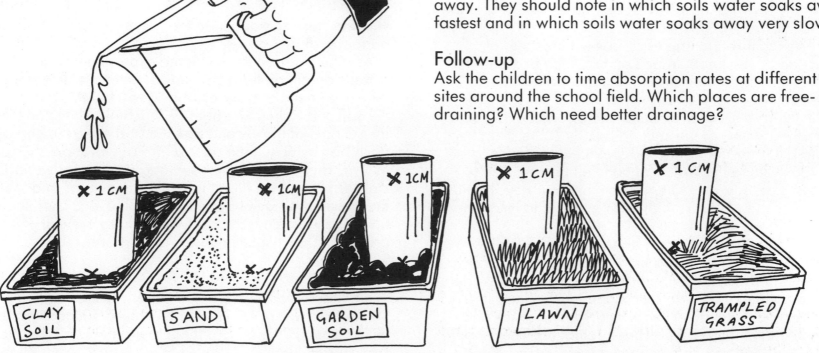

Soil erosion

Age range
Seven to eleven.

Group size
Groups of four.

What you need
Two same-size cardboard or wooden boxes 20cm x 40cm x 4cm deep, two sheets of plastic, 2 litre glass or plastic jars, a watering can, enough soil to fill each box, a stop-watch.

What to do
Explain that the purpose of this experiment is to determine how the angle of slope and contouring of the soil each affect soil erosion.

Tell the children to line each box with a sheet of plastic and cut a spout in one end of each box and its plastic liner. Then they should fill each box with the same soil.

The children should raise the end of one box by 6cm and raise the end of the second box by 15cm. They should put a jar under the spout at the opposite end of each box. Using the watering can, tell the children to add one litre of water to each box in turn. They should try to pour the water from the same height in the same way and at the same speed.

The children should time how long it takes for water to start dripping from the spouts. They should note which box drips first and describe how the colour of the water in each bottle varies. They should note how long it takes to fill each jar, then filter the water from each jar and measure how much soil has been removed. They should investigate if more soil has been removed from the box

with the steeper slope than the gentler slope. (This is the normal pattern.)

Ask the children to repeat the experiment with two boxes containing the same soil. This time, using a finger, they should make a series of ridges (contours) across the soil surface, each about 2–3cm high. They can leave the surface of the second box flat and raise the end of each box by 6cm, then pour a litre of water on each box in turn. They should time how long it takes for water to start dripping then filter the water in each jar and measure how much soil has been removed. They should investigate whether the contours help to prevent soil erosion. (They usually make a big difference.)

Follow-up
The children could repeat the experiment using two steeper slopes: one with the box raised 10cm and one with it raised 20cm and put contours on both soils. Do contours still help to reduce soil erosion?

Igneous rocks

Age range
Nine to eleven.

Group size
Pairs.

What you need
A collection of igneous (volcanic) rocks (such as granite (different colours), basalt and pumice stone); warm water, a magnifying glass, a copper coin, a steel nail.

What to do
Tell the children that the display shows a collection of igneous rocks. Explain the formation of igneous rocks from volcanic eruptions. Igneous rock starts as molten lava beneath the earth's crust. The lava reaches the surface through volcanoes and vents. The lava then cools and solidifies. If it cools slowly, large crystals form in the rock, for example, granite. If it cools quickly, only very small crystals form, for example, basalt. Lava which is full of air bubbles and which is thrown out of a volcano cools to form pumice – a rock with air bubbles trapped inside.

Ask the children to study each of the samples of igneous rock. Tell them to look at each through the magnifying glass. Can they see crystals? Get them to scratch each sample, first with the copper coin then with the steel nail. Which samples are marked by the coin? Which by neither the coin nor the nail? They should then put each sample in a basin of warm water. Which samples float? (Pumice is the only one.) Now tell them to hold that stone under water. What comes out of the stone? (Air bubbles.)

Follow-up
The children can repeat the experiments with different samples of igneous rocks. How far do the results match? Can they identify granite, basalt and pumice?

Sedimentary rocks

Age range
Nine to eleven.

Group size
Pairs.

What you need
A collection of sedimentary rocks (such as limestone, chalk, sandstone, mudstone), a magnifying glass, a copper coin, a steel nail, a glass jar, some white vinegar.

What to do
Tell the children that this display is a collection of sedimentary rocks. Explain how sedimentary rocks form in layers under water. They are made up of material deposited by rivers such as sand or mud. Other rocks like chalk and limestone are made of the skeletons and shells of ancient sea creatures.

Ask the children to study each of the samples of sedimentary rock. Can they see different layers in them? Now tell them to use a magnifying glass. Can they see the fossil remains of plants or animals? (These are best seen in limestone.) Tell the children to scratch each sample with the copper coin and the steel nail. Which is the hardest? Which is the softest? Ask them to put a small piece of each sample in the jar and cover it with vinegar. Which ones fizz and give off carbon dioxide? (Limestone and chalk.) Which piece dissolves fastest? (Chalk.)

Follow-up
Children could repeat the experiment using different samples of sedimentary rocks (such as gritstones) and different types of limestone (for example, oolitic, carboniferous). These samples can often be obtained from local secondary schools which have collections as well as local museums which may have rock collections. How far do the results differ?

Links with other curriculum areas

Art
- patterns in different types of rock, e.g., igneous and metamorphic.

Mathematics
- sorting;
- classifying.

Science
- properties of different materials including rocks and soil;
- rocks and soil and living organisms;
- experiments with different rocks and soils.

Rocks and soil

Technology
- designing and making fossils or series of rock strata to represent a model of an area, e.g., Grand Canyon.

History
- history of ancient life as revealed by fossils and peat or ice preservation.

English
- poems and stories about rocks, soil and the animals that live in the soil.

Volcanoes and earthquakes

Volcanoes and earthquakes together make some of the most dramatic world events. They feature in newspaper and television headlines and for a short time the world's media focus on a small part of the world. It is important to maximise the benefits of such events for the teaching and learning of geography. If it is not possible to undertake a project on earthquakes and volcanoes at short notice when the actual event takes place, try to collect newspaper and magazine accounts, together with video footage, for use at a later date. In this way you will be able to bring reality to teaching and learning about events in distant places. Focus on the accounts of real people, in real places, with which the children will be able to empathise.

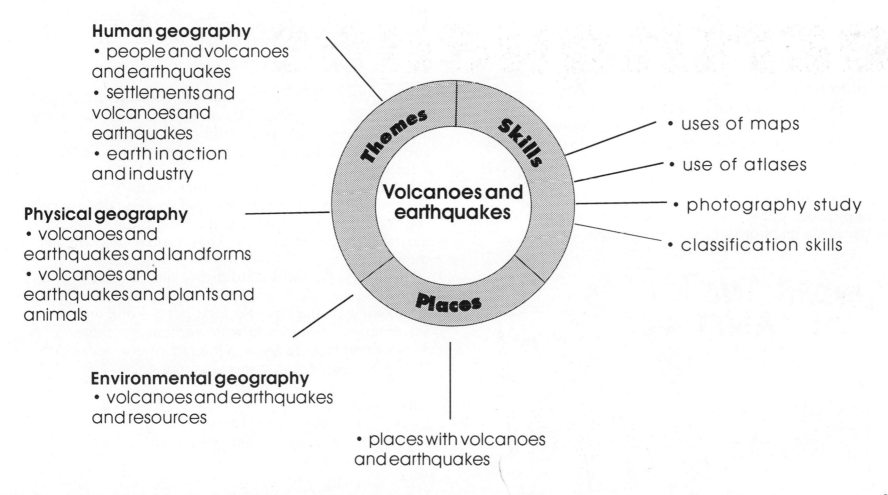

Human geography
- people and volcanoes and earthquakes
- settlements and volcanoes and earthquakes
- earth in action and industry

Physical geography
- volcanoes and earthquakes and landforms
- volcanoes and earthquakes and plants and animals

Environmental geography
- volcanoes and earthquakes and resources

Themes

Skills

Places

Volcanoes and earthquakes

- uses of maps
- use of atlases
- photography study
- classification skills

- places with volcanoes and earthquakes

Eruptions and 'quakes

Age range
Five to seven.

Group size
Pairs.

What you need
Photocopies of newspaper and magazine cuttings, pictures and photographs of earthquakes or erupting volcanoes, scissors, adhesive, a scrapbook, paper, pens.

What to do
Although this activity can be done at any time, it would be most valuable when there has been an earthquake or volcanic eruption in the recent news. Explain to the class that they are going to compile a scrapbook about earthquakes and volcanoes.

Ask the children to work in pairs and give each pair some pictures, photocopies of newspaper articles and magazines with photographs and accounts of an

earthquake or volcanic eruption. Encourage the children also to bring in material from home on other volcanoes or earthquakes, both past and present. The aim is for each pair to produce six or seven sheets to go in the class scrapbook.

The children should stick the pictures and photographs in the scrapbook and write a caption for each page, together with a brief description of what it shows. Younger children may need some help with the captions.

Encourage the children to draw their own picture illustrating the effects of the eruption or earthquake, in particular showing how it affects people and their environment. They should write captions for these pictures and include these in the scrapbook which can be kept in the reading corner for reference.

Follow-up
On a globe stick coloured symbols to show the location of some of the main volcanoes and earthquake areas, both past and present.

Make a volcano

Age range
Five to seven.

Group size
Groups of four.

What you need
A cardboard box about 30cm square, newspaper, adhesive, paint, water, brushes, photocopiable page 118 showing a volcano in cross-section, photographs of volcanoes erupting.

What to do
Discuss the photographs of erupting volcanoes. Give each child a copy of photocopiable page 118 and talk about how volcanoes create their cone shape and how they throw out ash, lava and even steam and gas. (The cone shape is made up of thousands of layers of ash and lava. The volcano is steep-sided at the centre because it is made of lava flows and coarse ash. Further away from the centre it is made up of finer layers of ash and thus the slope is less steep.)

Explain that the task is to make a volcano to show what it looks like when it is cut through. Ask the children to cut away one side of the box. Then they should soak the newspaper in adhesive to create papier mache. The children can build up layers of papier mache inside the box to create the cone shape. They must keep the front part flat as this will show the cross-section.

When the model is dry the children should paint the different layers of ash and lava on the front of the cone. They should add labels to show the crater, the ash and the lava.

Follow-up
Children can draw pictures to show how the volcano can change shape when it explodes, often blowing away the top or the sides.

The moving earth

Age range
Seven to eleven.

Group size
Groups of four.

What you need
Photographs and newspaper cuttings of volcanoes, volcanic eruptions and earthquakes both past and present, a blank world map, scissors, adhesive, coloured wool.

What to do
Explain to the children that they are going to investigate the dramatic events of volcanic eruptions and earthquakes. Give each group a set of photographs and newspaper cuttings. They have to prepare a written report on the information before them which answers the key questions:
- Where in the world did this event take place?
- When did this event take place?
- What were the immediate effects of the event on people, animals and the environment?
- What were the longer term (after a month) effects of the event?
- What do local people think about it?
- What do experts say about the event?
- What were the causes of the eruption or the earthquake?
- What has happened to the area since the event, i.e. how far have things returned to normal?
- Why do people continue to live in places where earthquakes and volcanic eruptions are quite common?

Each group can produce a wall display of photographs, newspaper cuttings and their report based on the key questions. The eruptions and earthquakes should be located on the world map and linked to the appropriate part of the display by coloured wool.

Follow-up
Each group can give a brief verbal summary of its findings to the rest of the class, followed by a whole-class discussion comparing how different countries reacted to the same problem.

Earthquake!

Age range
Seven to eleven.

Group size
Groups of six.

What you need
Two pieces of card each 60cms x 30cms, cereal and other cardboard boxes, paper, paint, scissors.

What to do
Get the children to make simple buildings using the cereal and other boxes. Aim for different types of buildings, such as houses, some with flat roofs, others with pitched roofs. Include taller buildings such as blocks of flats and offices.

Let the children arrange the buildings in the form of a village or small town by standing them on the two sheets of card. Ask the groups to paint in a river flowing through the settlement together with roads and bridges.

Next explain that during an earthquake the ground moves violently and often large cracks open up. Then simulate an earthquake on the village by moving the cards at the base of the model rapidly backwards and forwards, just as the ground would move during earthquake vibrations. The children should watch carefully what happens to all the buildings in their village, as well as to the stream and to the roads. Then they should draw pictures with captions to record how the village looks after the earthquake. They should redesign and remake buildings which are better able to withstand an earthquake, such as being able to sway with the quake or being lower and stronger. Then repeat the earthquake and test the newly-designed buildings.

Follow-up
Children can draw and paint pictures which illustrate the features of buildings which allow them to survive an earthquake.

Volcanoes around the world

Age range
Nine to eleven.

Group size
Groups of three or four.

What you need
A list of volcanoes around the world with their latitude and longitude and dates of eruption, a blank world map (see photocopiable page 116. Draw lines of latitude and longitude on the master copy.), a computer database, reference books.

What to do
Get the children to plot the volcanoes on photocopiable page 116, using latitude and longitude to locate each one. They should also record the name of the country in which each volcano is to be found.

Using the computer program and reference books, ask the children to set up a volcano database. Tell them to include the name of the volcano, the date(s) when it erupted and the country in which it is located. Additional information about the volcanoes, such as their height and numbers of people killed, can be obtained from reference books and added to the database.

Get the children to interrogate the programe to answer key questions such as:
● Which was the most recent volcano to erupt?
● Which country has the largest number of volcanoes?
● Which country has the highest volcano?
● Which volcano killed the largest number of people?
● How many people have died in volcanic eruptions since 1900?

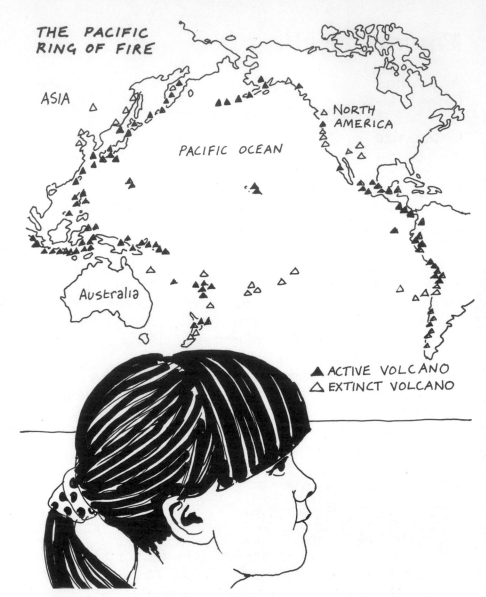

Follow-up
The children could investigate why some volcanoes create massive destruction and loss of life, yet others create relatively little damage.

Mount St Helens

Age range
Nine to eleven.

Group size
Whole class.

What you need
Photocopiable page 119 describing the Mount St Helens eruption in 1980, an atlas, paper, pens.

What to do
Explain to the children that they will be studying one volcanic eruption, namely Mount St Helens in the state of Washington in the USA. Ask the children to locate Washington state and Mount St Helens. Of which range of mountains does Mount St Helens form a part? (the Cascade range) What other volcanic peaks can the children find in the same range of mountains? (Rainier, Mount Hood, Mount Adams)

Give each child photocopiable page 119 describing the Mount St Helens eruption. Talk about the eruption in terms of:
- the explosion, gas, ash and flames;
- loss of life;
- damage to the environment, i.e. trees, rivers, lakes;
- damage to people's homes.

Get the children to compile lists of the main problems facing people who lived close to Mount St Helens as a result of the eruption. They can also use the photocopiable sheet as the basis for creative writing involving narrow escapes from death or a personalised account of someone at the scene.

Follow-up
Get the children to compare the eruption of Mount St Helens with another eruption, such as that in Pompeii in AD 27.

Life must go on

Age range
Nine to eleven.

Group size
Whole class working in groups.

What you need
Photocopiable page 120 which describes the effects of the Mexico City earthquake of 1985.

What to do
Explain that the aim of the activity is to examine the effects of a large earthquake on a major city by studying the case of Mexico City. In particular, point out that the intention is to highlight the problems created for the people of the city and how groups and individuals reacted to the disaster.

Get the children to read photocopiable page 120 describing some of the immediate effects of the earthquake. Divide the class into groups representing the different services which have responsibility for helping the people of the city after the earthquake, for example:
- medical staff – doctors, nurses;
- police;
- gas authority;
- water and sewage authority;
- electricity authority;
- telephone company;
- fire service;
- ambulance service;
- traffic department;
- emergency rescue teams (with dogs and heavy moving equipment);
- radio and TV;
- city mayor's office.

Ask the children in each group to draw up a list of actions they would seek to take after the earthquake. They should then prioritise the list starting with the most urgent and consider which other groups they would need to seek help from.

Then ask each group to read their list of priorities to the rest of the class and encourage the other groups to comment on aspects, such as how *they* might help or which sections of the community should get help first and how this should be organised. Let the whole class discuss the varied roles of each group, such as the need for regular radio and TV bulletins to let people know what is happening and what to expect or the need for the police to prevent looting and aid the movement of rescue teams around the city.

> Order of priorities
> 1. Emergency rescue.
> 2. Restore electricity and lines of communication.

When they have done this, ask the children to write an account of how their group could best respond to a disaster like the one in Mexico City and what preparations the group could make, such as practising evacuating buildings.

Follow-up
Ask the children to compare the effects of the Mexico City earthquake with those of others, such as Armenia in 1989, San Francisco in 1989, or India in 1993.

Links with other curriculum areas

Art
- the sounds and moods of earth in action.

English
- stories and poems about famous earthquakes (e.g. San Francisco 1906) and volcanoes (e.g. Krakatoa).

Science
- volcanoes and plate tectonics and the structure of the earth;
- Properties of materials.

Volcanoes and earthquakes

Technology
- designing and making buildings to resist earthquake damage.

History
- importance of volcanic eruptions and earthquakes in history (e.g. Pompeii).

Mathematics
- sorting volcanoes into different types — active, dormant, extinct.

Weather

While weather remains a popular topic in most schools, not least because of its links with science, there remain some aspects which still suffer neglect. In particular, the geographical dimension of contrasting weather in different parts of the world often receives scant treatment at Key Stage 2. Yet children's curiosity about the weather experienced by different places around the world is often aroused at an early age and continues to increase. One reason for this is the growth of travel, with more children taking holidays in places with different weather. Another reason for this interest is the high profile that weather around the world receives on television, especially its adverse effects, such as hurricanes, floods, avalanches or tornadoes.

The activities in this chapter provide a practical way of introducing children to the idea of different types of weather around the world, without the necessity of a field trip to experience such different weather! Thus the activities provide a lively substitute for children who will not be able to discover the weather in different places at first hand.

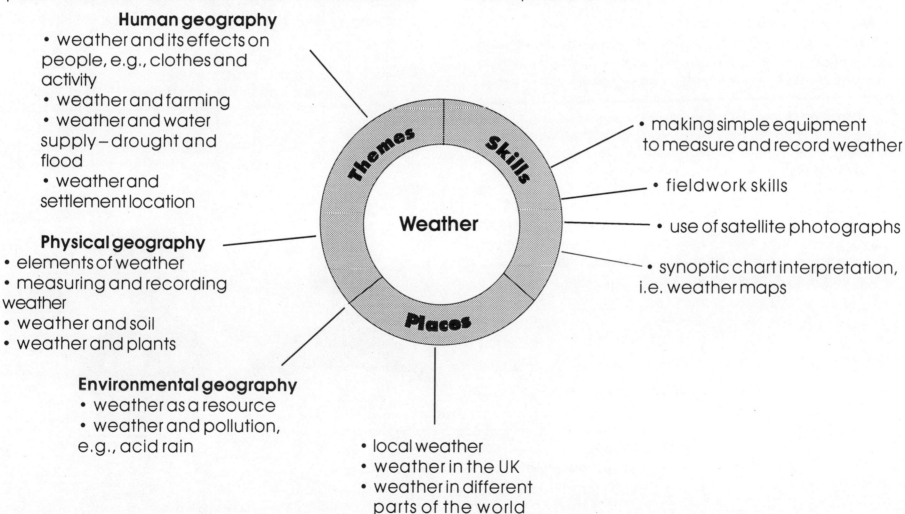

Human geography
• weather and its effects on people, e.g., clothes and activity
• weather and farming
• weather and water supply – drought and flood
• weather and settlement location

Physical geography
• elements of weather
• measuring and recording weather
• weather and soil
• weather and plants

Environmental geography
• weather as a resource
• weather and pollution, e.g., acid rain

Themes

Skills

Weather

Places

• making simple equipment to measure and record weather

• fieldwork skills

• use of satellite photographs

• synoptic chart interpretation, i.e. weather maps

• local weather
• weather in the UK
• weather in different parts of the world

Raindrops

Age range
Five to seven.

Group size
Groups of four or pairs.

What you need
A biscuit tin or similar lid about 24cms x 16cms, some plain flour, a sieve, a magnifying glass for each group, paper, pencils and a simple plan of the school.

What to do
Show the children how to make a raindrop collector by carefully filling the tin lid with flour. During a rain shower get them to put the raindrop collectors outside the classroom in different places around the school; for instance, in the open, under a tree, close to a wall. The collectors should be left for a few minutes (five in steady drizzle, less in a heavy downpour). Tell the children to give each collector a number and to mark theirs on a simple plan of the school.

They should bring the collectors indoors and allow the flour to dry for about five minutes before putting it through a fine sieve. The shape of some of the raindrops will be preserved in the flour. Now ask them to study each raindrop with a magnifying glass. What shape is it? Ask them to draw the shape.

How do the shape and size of the raindrops collected in other parts of the school differ from those collected in the open? Are the drops bigger or smaller? Are they the same shape?

Other key questions to ask are:
- Which collector had most pellets?
- Which collector had the fewest pellets?

Follow-up
During a rainstorm, collectors could be used to compare the size and shape of raindrops at the start, middle and end of the storm.

The raindrop collector

Weather and clothes

Age range
Five to seven.

Group size
Whole class in four groups.

What you need
A range of clothing suitable for different seasons, for example, woollen scarves, gloves, socks, hats, coats, leggings, cotton T-shirts, shorts, sandals, swimsuit, thin anoraks, wellingtons, fur-lined boots; a cardboard box, four tables labelled winter, spring, summer and autumn.

What to do
Put all the clothing in a box in the centre of the room. Discuss how the weather affects the clothes we wear, for example we wear more layers and heavier clothing in cold weather. Discuss how the weather changes during the year. Stress the importance of spring and autumn, as well as the contrasts between summer and winter.

Ask the children to take turns to select an item of clothing from the box. They can then discuss with the rest of the class for which season it is most appropriate. The children should think carefully about the spring and autumn weather when there is a need for a mixture of warm and cool clothing.

Once the items have been allocated to a season, children can examine the results and decide what other clothing should be included for that season (for example, sports equipment).

Follow-up
Children could record their results pictorially by drawing pictures to represent scenes and activities associated with each of the seasons, and creating a border of appropriate clothing around each.

A seasonal scene

Age range
Five to seven.

Group size
Groups of four.

What you need
A length of wall display board divided into the four seasons, cotton wool, tissue paper, frieze paper, paints, crayons, scissors, adhesive.

What to do
Draw the outline of the same scene on each of the four sections of wall board. The scene should include a large tree (deciduous), a mountain, a lake and a river.

Ask the children to complete each scene for the appropriate season. Discuss beforehand what would be seen on the tree (for example, yellow leaves in autumn, pale green in spring, dark green in summer), as well as the mountain (snow in winter, bare rock on the top in spring and autumn, grass in summer) and the lake (frozen in winter with people skating, danger signs in spring and autumn and people boating or swimming in summer). Similarly, the river may be large and brown in spring as the snow melts, blue in summer (with swimmers, fishermen, people paddling), grey or brown in autumn with floods, and have white frozen edges in winter.

Other aspects to consider are blossom on the tree in spring, snow on the tree branches in winter, birds in the tree in spring and summer, animals such as a squirrel in the tree in spring, summer and autumn.

Follow-up
Children can add the weather of a typical day to each season, for example high winds in autumn, frost or snow in winter, rain in spring and sunshine in summer.

Clues to the season

Age range
Five to seven.

Group size
Whole class.

What you need
A set of clue cards for winter, spring, summer and autumn. Each clue card should contain a related word or words and a picture to illustrate the point. Some examples of key words are:

Winter	Spring	Summer	Autumn
Frost	Tadpoles	Big green	Falling leaves
Snow	Showers	leaves	Storms
Ice	Buds	Sunshine	Fog
Sledge	New leaves	Swimming	Harvest
Scarf	Lambs	Cricket	Conkers
Dark nights	Daffodils	Holiday	Dew
Skiing	Blossom	Seaside	Berries
	Cuckoo	Light nights	Birds flying away

What to do
Arrange the classroom with four large tables or display boards representing each of the seasons. A child (dressed in the clothes appropriate for each season) should be in charge of each table.

Each child selects a card from a central box and reads it out and/or shows it to the rest of the class. The class then discuss on which table they think the card should be placed.

Follow-up
The children can each make their own record of the words relating to each season and add any further words they can think of. They might like to take their lists home to see if parents or carers can add an appropriate word.

Weather around the world

Age range
Seven to nine.

Group size
Pairs.

What you need
Photographs of weather in different parts of the world, e.g. sunshine on Mediterranean beaches, a frozen scene in winter in Moscow, heavy rain in India or Pakistan, a thunderstorm in Britain, a hurricane in the Caribbean. Some photographs can come from travel brochures, others from magazines and advertisements. A large blank world map, an atlas, coloured wool, drawing pins.

What to do
Give one child in each pair a photograph. This child should look carefully at it but conceal it from the second child. Tell the first child to describe the picture in as much detail as possible, mentioning people, animals, clothes, skies, clouds and any other clues as to what the weather is like. The second child must then draw the picture unseen from these instructions. The drawing and the photograph are then compared and the results discussed. What was left out? What was badly described? What features were added?

Children should then use an atlas to locate the place in the photograph and mount it on the wall near to the world map. They should use a piece of coloured wool to link each photograph with the places on the map.

Follow-up
Each pair of children can reverse the procedure with a second photograph, or alternatively can make a list of key points about the weather shown, for example, Is it wet or dry? Is it hot or cold? Is it windy or calm? How would the weather condition affect life in this place?

Weather hazards

Age range
Seven to eleven.

Group size
Groups of four.

What you need
Newspaper photographs and reports on weather events around the world (such as floods, droughts, thunderstorms and snowfalls), a world map, coloured wool, drawing pins.

What to do
Get the children to study the photographs and to read the accounts of weather hazards from around the world. Include some UK examples to reinforce the idea that these weather hazards and disasters happen all over the world, not solely in economically-developing countries.

Ask the children to locate on a world map where the disaster took place. Talk about how the events affected the lives of people living in that area. Mount the photographs on the wall around the world map and use coloured wool to link the event with the corresponding country.

The children should research in the school library (or on a visit to the local reference library) other weather events and disasters which have affected the UK and in particular the local area in the past. Do some places in the UK seem to suffer from the weather on a regular basis? Where are these places? What are the commonest hazards?

Now ask the children to pretend that they are eyewitness reporters recounting a major weather event in the UK, or, if they prefer, in an economically developing country. (If so, they may need to research this further.) What is the event? Where did it happen? What has caused it? How has it affected farms, schools, roads, railways, factories? They should consider the extent of damage, what is being done to overcome the resulting difficulties and what action could be taken in the future to limit the damage potential of such an event.

Evaporation rates

Age range
Seven to eleven.

Group size
Groups of two or three.

What you need
Two paper towels, a bowl of water, two metre rulers, drawing pins.

What to do
Tell the class that this activity is part of the investigation of the microclimate of the school and its grounds. Explain that the microclimate is the immediate local climate (conditions) around a particular site, for example, a school. This would include those places which are windy, those which are cold and those which are wet. A study of the microclimate would involve looking at these factors and how they change throughout the year. Discuss the fact that wet paper towels will dry out at different rates depending on the conditions; for example, one on a radiator will dry out much faster than one on the floor. Discuss the range of factors which are likely to affect the speed with which paper towels dry out; for example, will they dry out faster on a cloudy or a sunny day? Are they likely to dry out faster outdoors or indoors on a windy day?

Get the children to make an evaporation gauge by wetting two paper towels, then squeezing them until they are damp, then pinning one to the top of the two metre rulers and the other to the bottom (see opposite).

The children, working in groups, should position their evaporation gauges at various points both indoors and outdoors around the school grounds (for example,

under a hedge, against a wall, on a tarmac playing area) and record the time taken to dry and how drying-out times vary between upper and lower towels. They can use a record sheet like the one shown below.

Drying times	Start time	When dry	Time taken to dry
Upper towel			
Lower towel			

Follow-up
The children can try recording drying times in different locations at different times of the day, in different weather conditions and in different seasons.

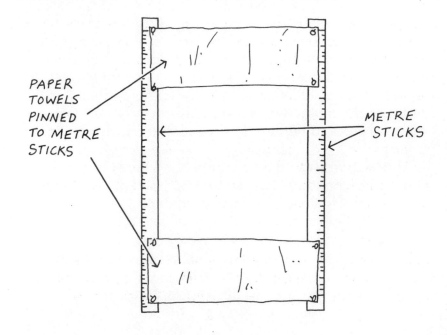

PAPER TOWELS PINNED TO METRE STICKS

METRE STICKS

Make a wind vane

Age range
Seven to eleven.

Group size
Pairs.

What you need
Stiff card, a plastic straw, a plastic bottle, Plasticine, a large headed pin, a rubber-ended pencil, sticky tape, scissors, a compass.

What to do
Children can make their own wind vanes using the following instructions:
- Cut out two triangles from card, one bigger than the other (e.g. one 8cm per side, one 12cm per side).
- Use tape to stick the larger triangle to one end of the straw as the tail and the smaller triangle to the opposite end of the straw as the point (see diagram opposite).
- Pin the straw in the middle to the end of the rubber-ended pencil. Fix the pencil into a hole in the bottom of a plastic bottle with some Plasticine.
- Place the wind vane in the school grounds and use the compass to mark the eight main directions – N, NE, E, SE, S, SW, W, NW, having found out where the north point is beforehand. The arrow will point to the direction from which the wind is blowing.

Follow-up
Tell the children to place the wind vane in different positions around the school on the same day. Does the wind blow from the same direction at each place?

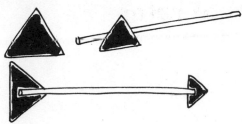

1. Stick larger triangle at one end of the straw, the smaller one to the other end, both pointing the same way.

2. Pin the straw in the middle to the end of a rubber-ended pencil.

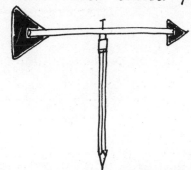

3. Fix the pencil in Plasticine inside the plastic bottle.

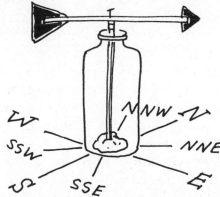

Make an anemometer

Age range
Nine to eleven.

Group size
Pairs.

What you need
Two pieces of wood 10cm x 20cm x 1cm, adhesive, a piece of dowelling 1cm in diameter and 10cm long, string, a piece of light card 8cm square, scissors, a protractor, a marker pen.

What to do
The children can make their own anemometer using the following instructions:
● Stick the two pieces of wood together at right angles (as shown in the diagram).
● Stick the dowelling to the upright piece of wood.
● Thread two pieces of string through holes in the top of the card and attach the string loosely to the dowelling.
● Use the protractor and pen to mark every 10° as a scale on the upright piece of wood.
● Now place the anemometer in a wind spot. Note how far along the scale the piece of card rises.
   The children should use these angles to calculate the speed of the wind:

Angle	90°	80°	70°	60°	50°	40°	30°	20°	10°
Wind speed in km/h	0	13	19	24	29	34	41	52	77

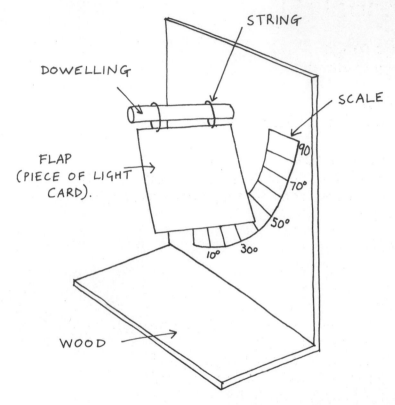

A flap anemometer

Follow-up
Tell the children to record the wind speed at different places around the school. Where is the wind strongest? Where is there least breeze? This task could be related to siting a bench for sitting out in summer.

Temperatures around school (1)

Age range
Nine to eleven.

Group size
Whole class divided into four groups.

What you need
Four spirit thermometers, four cardboard tubes from inside kitchen rolls, tin foil, masking tape, Blu-tack, a compass.

What to do
Explain that the purpose of the experiment is to examine the ways in which temperature varies at different points around the school exterior. Ensure that children are able to read a thermometer, and then provide them with the following instructions:
• Wrap the cardboard tubes in tin foil.
• Tape the tubes to four of the outside walls of the school building facing different directions and fix the thermometer inside with Blu-tack.
• Locate the tubes about a metre above the ground. The foil wrapped tubes will reflect any sunlight and allow air to circulate freely around the thermometer so ensuring more accurate results.
• Record the temperature of each thermometer after ten minutes.
• Continue to record the temperature of each thermometer every hour. Use the results to draw graphs of temperature change on each wall.
Some key questions for the children to investigate are:

• Which wall showed the greatest changes in temperature during the day?
• On which wall did the temperature stay mostly the same?
• Which wall had the highest temperature for the longest time?
• In which direction would you prefer your classroom to face?

Follow-up
The experiment can be repeated on four different exterior walls. How far do the results differ? Repeat the experiment at a different time of year. Do the results change significantly?

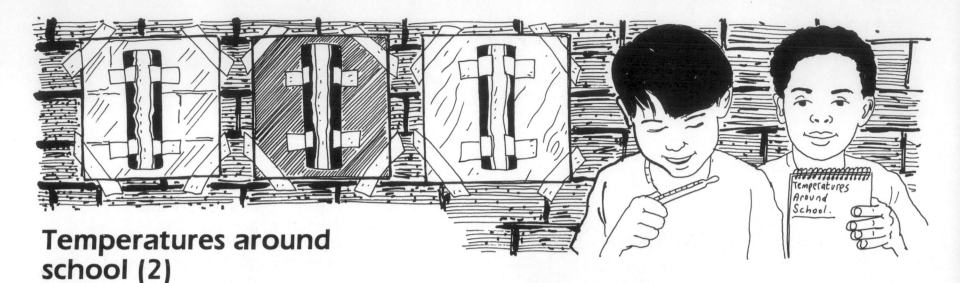

Temperatures around school (2)

Age range
Nine to eleven.

Group size
Whole class working in four groups.

What you need
Four spirit thermometers, four cardboard tubes from the inside of kitchen rolls, tin foil, masking tape, Blu-tack, a piece of wood 50cm square, a piece of glass 50cm square and a piece of metal 50cm square.

What to do
Explain that the purpose of the experiment is to examine how temperatures in the school grounds vary according to the nature of the wall surface. Ensure that the children are able to read a thermometer, and then provide them with the following instructions:
• Place the pieces of wood, glass and metal in line against the brick wall.

• Wrap the cardboard tubes in foil.
• Tape one tube on to each of the surfaces along the same wall at the same height, for example, a metre above the ground.
• Fix a thermometer inside each tube with Blu-tack.
• Record the temperature of each thermometer after ten minutes, and then every hour.
• Use the data to draw graphs of the temperature changes over the day for each of the different surfaces.
  Some of the key questions for the children to investigate are:
  • Which surface heated up fastest?
  • Which surface showed most variation in temperature during the day?
  • Which surface became the warmest?
  • Which surface remained coolest all day?

Follow-up
The experiment can be repeated using the same materials but on a wall facing in a different direction. What are the main changes?

Links with other curriculum areas

History
- weather events in the past, e.g. freezing of the Thames, Great Gale, whirlwinds.

Art
- pictures of different weather conditions and related aspects such as high winds, blizzards, sunsets.

Music
- different types of music related to different weather conditions, e.g. thunder, calm, tropical heat.

Weather

Science and technology
- designing and making simple instruments for measuring wind speed, wind direction and temperature variations around the school grounds;
- seasonal change.

Mathematics
- work on graphs related to temperature, wind speed and wind direction.

English
- weather in literature;
- poems and stories about weather;
- weather sayings, e.g. Red sky at night, shepherd's delight.

PE
- moving in different ways, e.g. in a gale, in a blizzard, in hot weather.

Water resources

Water is one of the most common themes in primary education. The more general projects on water described here are primarily geared to the infant age-range because, in the Geography National Curriculum Programme of Study, water at Key Stage One naturally leads on to rivers at Key Stage Two. Hence this approach has been adopted in this chapter.

Work on water lends itself to lots of practical activities, some of which may be classroom-based, but others require an outdoor setting. For this reason many teachers choose the summer term to study water. Water play naturally lends itself to projects in maths but there is also scope for geographical work linked to play as this section describes. The links between geography and science are particularly close in water projects and this is one of the advantages in choosing such a project. However, care must be taken to ensure a balance between geographical projects, as outlined here, and more science-based ones such as sinking and floating.

Work on rivers is in many ways a natural progression from that on water at Key Stage 1. It is important to develop practical hands-on projects which involve the children in carrying out simple experiments in sand trays. This practical work is a significant part of geographical enquiry – that is, encouraging the children to ask questions and to formulate hypotheses which can then be investigated through the practical projects. Such work will then provide a balance with the more traditional approaches to rivers, which focus on how rivers are used, for example, to provide hydro-electricity or irrigation or to provide places for leisure.

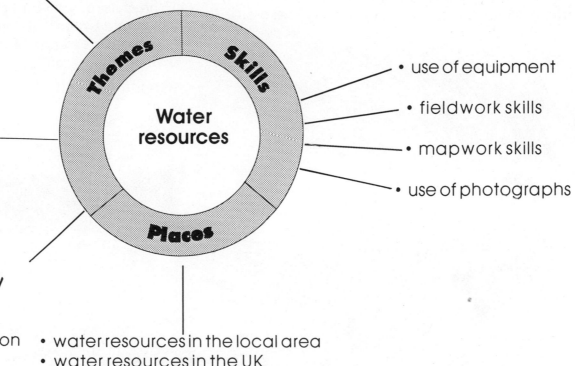

Human geography
• people and water resources, e.g., flood
• water and settlements, e.g., location of rivers, slope of land and so on

Physical geography
• weather and water resources
• water and landforms
• water and erosion; transport and deposition

Environmental geography
• obtaining water resources
• pollution and conservation of water resources

Water resources

Themes

Skills
• use of equipment
• fieldwork skills
• mapwork skills
• use of photographs

Places
• water resources in the local area
• water resources in the UK and other parts of the world

Water around us

Age range
Five to seven.

Group size
Whole class.

What you need
Photographs of water in the landscape (for example, rivers, streams, lakes, seas, estuaries, waterfalls, clouds, ponds, reservoirs, thunderstorms and/or heavy rain, snowfall, fog, frost, mist, people washing, people drinking, a car wash, swimming, water skiing, sailing, boats); frieze paper, card, paints, adhesive, scissors.

What to do
Talk about the many different ways we find water around us, especially in the landscape as rivers, ponds, streams, waterfalls, lakes and seas. Include ideas about how people use water in the landscape for sports such as sailing and windsurfing as well as for washing and drinking. Extend the idea of water around us to include rain, hail, sleet, snow, fog and frost.

The children should then make a large collage to show water in its many different forms. Ask them to write labels for each scene and stick them on the correct part of the collage.

Follow-up
The children can add pictures to the collage which illustrate water in its different forms from around the world, for example Victoria Falls, the river Nile, Lake Michigan.

Soil, pebbles, sand and water

Age range
Five to nine.

Group size
Whole class divided into three groups.

What you need
Three separate piles of sand, pebbles and soil each about half a metre high in the school grounds, a watering can with a rose for each group.

What to do
Explain to the children that water is capable of moving materials like sand, pebbles and soil. The three processes involved are *erosion*, that is, the removal of material, *transport*, that is, the movement of the eroded material, and *deposition*, that is, the dropping off of the eroded material. This terminology should be used with discretion by the teacher but certainly by age seven, most children should be familiar with these terms.

Give each group a watering can with two litres of water in it. Ask a member of each group to pour the water slowly from the can using the rose to give a light stream of water. Ensure that the children pour the water from the same height at the same speed over each type of material.

Ask the other group members to note carefully what happens to the sand, the soil and the pebbles and then the groups can compare results at the end. What evidence is there that material is being eroded, transported and deposited? How far does the water spread? What is the colour of the water at the end of the activity? Is more sand removed than soil or pebbles?

How far are the sand, soil and pebbles transported before they are deposited? Ask older children to write a description of the experiment, focussing on the evidence they saw of erosion, transport and deposition.

Follow-up
Repeat the experiments using either four litres of water or two litres of water poured without the rose. How do the results differ?

Floods

Age range
Seven to nine.

Group size
Groups of four.

What you need
Photographs of floods and flooding from around the world together with newspaper reports and video tapes of news bulletins.

What to do
Explain to the class that the aim is to examine floods in different parts of the world. Each group should study some photographs and newspaper cuttings of a particular flood and then consider the following questions:
• Where was the flood?
• What was the cause of the flood?
• What were the effects of the flood on: buildings; people; animals; roads and vehicles?
• How long did the flood last?
• What is now being done to prevent future floods?

The groups should then write a report based on their analysis of the pictures and cuttings.

Each group should make a presentation to the rest of the class – this should include the report, some accompanying photographs and simple diagrams displayed on the board if necessary. The rest of the class can ask questions about the flooding.

After the presentation the children should draw conclusions about the places which are most vulnerable to floods. Are they always places close to the coast? Are they near rivers? Are they very flat? Which parts of the world do not seem to suffer from floods? Why do they think this is?

Follow-up
Children should summarise measures taken in different parts of the world to prevent floods in the future, such as building dams or embankments. Which seems to be most successful?

The island

Age range
Seven to nine.

Group size
Whole class.

What you need
Frieze paper, sugar paper, pictures of rivers, waterfalls, lakes, swamps, seas, coasts; scissors, adhesive, pencils, crayons, marker pens.

What to do
This activity has a 'Treasure Island' theme. Let the children study pictures of rivers (different sizes and different parts of a river, for example, near its source and near its mouth), waterfalls, lakes, swamps, coasts and seas. Then talk about drawing a map of an imaginary island with these features on which treasure is buried near a river.

The children should each draw the outline of their own treasure island taking care to include all the key water features they have studied in the pictures. The map can show the features in either pictorial or symbol form, but in each case the features should be clearly labelled. The children should give each feature a name such as Spirit Lake, Boulder River, Last Chance Swamp, Dead Man's Cave, Eagle Falls. Make sure that the features relate to real landscapes, for example, the river might flow from the mountains, via a lake to the sea and get wider as it does so.

The map can then form the basis of activities using letter number grids to locate the treasure. Ask the children to write down a set of secret, detailed instructions outlining the route to the treasure. The aim

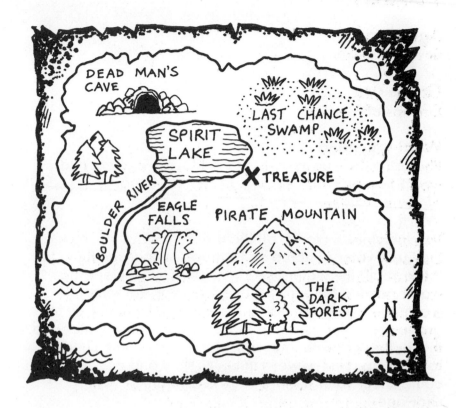

here is to combine map work with descriptions of river features, for example, 'Start at the mouth of the river at A5, then paddle inland through B4 and C5 until you reach the waterfall. The children should decide exactly where their treasure is buried and then get a friend to follow a route to find it.

Follow-up
The map can form the basis of additional work on maps such as symbols, use of the eight point compass or four figure grid references.

Using water

Age range
Seven to eleven.

Group size
Whole class.

What you need
Photocopiable page 121 for each pupil, posters and pamphlets on water supply in the local area.

What to do
Ask the children to list all the different ways in which they use water at home and school. Encourage them to think about the water used in each activity. Does the water need to be pure for every activity, for example washing the car or cleaning teeth? Ask the children to group the water uses into those needing pure water and those possible with impure water. Now tell the children to draw up a list of ways in which they and their families could save water if there were a drought or water shortage.

Next, use photocopiable page 121 to explain the water cycle from clouds in the sky to taps in their homes. Ask the children to colour the pictures, cut them out and arrange them in a logical sequence, then write in their own words a brief explanation of the sequence.

Follow-up
Contact your local water company for information about the local water supply. Where are the reservoirs and pumping stations? Where are the sewage works? Why is all water purified? How is water purified? In addition, the children can draw bar graphs showing how much water each person in the UK uses every day based on these figures:

Cooking and drinking	4 litres per person
Washing clothes	14 litres per person
Bath or shower	15 litres per person
Lavatory	34 litres per person

Reservoirs

Age range
Seven to eleven.

Group size
Whole class.

What you need
Photographs of reservoirs in the UK or abroad, pamphlets and leaflets about local reservoirs from the local water company (most provide educational information packs), photocopiable page 122, pictures of different water-based activities, for example, sailing (powered and non-powered), fishing, swimming, windsurfing, canoeing, rowing; atlases showing rainfall distribution in the UK, an OS map of the chosen area.

What to do
Tell the children to study the atlas map of UK annual rainfall. Where are the wettest areas? What are the names of these wettest zones? Why do they think these areas get so much rain and snow?

The teacher should choose a local reservoir and ask the children to make a detailed study of it. Is it situated in a particularly wet area of the UK? They should use the leaflets and Ordnance Survey map to describe the reservoir. How long is it? How wide is it? Which area does it serve? What is the nearest town?

The children should refer to the information leaflets and pamphlets to discover how much the reservoir is used for activities other than water storage, such as windsurfing, fishing, canoeing or other water sports.

Now give each child a copy of photocopiable page 122 and distribute the pictures of water-based activities round the class. The children should consider how the area can be opened up for water sports. Where would they build a car park, a toilet block, a caravan site, a restaurant and a picnic area? They should mark these on the map, then write down their reasons for each choice. What points should have been taken into consideration?

Follow-up
Discuss with the children why some people might object to changing the area by opening it up for water sports. Hold a class debate on the issue and then vote at the end of it.

53

Slopes and water

Age range
Nine to eleven.

Group size
Groups of five.

What you need
A measuring tape, a ruler, clipboards, paper, pens, graph paper.

What to do
Explain that the aim of the activity is to measure slopes in roads to establish how water drains away from the surface.

Choose a quiet street and station two pupils to watch for traffic and warn the three making and recording the measurements of approaching vehicles. Stretch the measuring tape tightly across the street from top of kerb to top of kerb.

With a ruler, the third pupil should measure the distance down from the measuring tape to the road surface. These measurements should be taken every 60cm across the road.

Back in the classroom the children should use the data to draw a cross-section on graph paper to show how the height of the road changes. They should show where the highest point is across the road (usually in the centre). Other points to consider are: the lowest point (usually at the kerb side); the nearest drain and how the design of the road promotes good drainage.

Follow-up
The children should carry out the same survey on different streets or within the school playground. Do all streets have the same slopes? What is the slope of the playground? Is there a drain at the base of the slope?

Drought

Age range
Nine to eleven.

Group size
Pairs.

What you need
Pictures/photographs of drought conditions in the UK and other countries (e.g., dried-up reservoirs, trees or grass on fire, dried-up water holes, animals dead from drought, sun-baked, cracked earth crops dried up, people starving); newspaper cuttings of drought, reference books, a blank world map, scissors, adhesive.

What to do
Explain the background to drought, which is a long spell of dry weather. In Britain this is fifteen consecutive days each with less than 0.25mm of rainfall. Drought affected Britain in 1976, 1984, 1989. However, it mainly affects other countries of the world, especially those in Africa close to the Sahara desert.

In pairs the children should study the pictures, newspaper cuttings and reference books in relation to drought in one particular country or one part of the world. The key questions to investigate are:
● Where is the country or area affected by drought?
● How long did the drought last?
● Does drought often affect this area?
● What are the main effects of drought on (1) people, (2) animals, (3) crops, (4) water supplies and (5) the landscape?
● What did governments do to conserve water or to reduce the amount used?
● What are people doing to try and prevent future problems with drought? (Building new reservoirs.)

Each pair should give a short presentation to the rest of the class describing the area of drought they have studied using the questions above. Then they can produce a wall display using the reference material, the information they have found and the map of the world showing the area. Major similarities and differences around the world are then highlighted. Are there common factors to the locations studied?

Follow-up
Ask the children to suggest ways of conserving water in their own immediate environment (for example 'Turn off the tap when you have finished' signs in the classroom, using water twice at home – once for car-washing then for flowers/grass, rain-water collecting tanks and so on).

The course of a river

Age range
Nine to eleven.

Group size
Groups of six.

What you need
A plastic tray 2m x 1m x 6cm (e.g., a classroom storage tray) with one of the shorter sides removed, sand, a watering can with a rose, a plastic bucket, two house bricks.

What to do
Tell the children to place the plastic tray on a bench then put the two house bricks under one end to create a slope down to the open end. They should put the plastic bucket under the open end to catch any sand and water. Now tell them to fill the tray with sand.

The aim of the activity is to create the pattern of a river flowing across the sandy landscape. The children can create sand mountains and other landscape features in different parts of the tray. At the raised end of the tray the children should slowly pour about two litres of water from the watering can using the rose. They should pour the water slowly so as not to wash away the sand suddenly.

The water will flow down the slope and start to create a channel. The children should note the shape of the channel and any points along it where they can see sand being eroded by the water and carried along by it.

They should note how the shape of the river channel changes when it meets sand hills or where it crosses flat areas, and be aware of any bends or meanders which start to form. In particular, children should notice how the water wears away the sand on the outside edge of a bend and deposits it on the inside edge.

Follow-up
This sand tray activity can be varied in many ways. Let the children try pouring more water for a longer period of time and see how the shape and size of the river channel changes. Then they can pour the water faster and create flood conditions and note how much more erosion takes place and at which points along the course of your river. Alternatively, tell the children to put a stone across the course of the river and note how the water builds up behind it in a lake before escaping round the side. Let them try to create a waterfall using 'rocks' across the whole tray. Notice how the sand is eroded at the foot of the waterfall in the *plunge pool*. These exercises will gain relevance if the children have an opportunity to experience the real thing first hand.

Local river study

Age range
Nine to eleven.

Group size
Groups of four.

What you need
Ordnance Survey maps 1:50,000 or1:25,000 of the local area which show rivers and streams; tracing paper, scissors, frieze paper, adhesive.

What to do
Give out the OS maps, one between two children. Explain that the task is to study rivers in the local area. Ask the children to study the key to the map and examine the symbols used to show rivers, lakes, marshes, bridges, footbridges, weirs, tidal limits and waterfalls.

Give each group an area of the map to study. In some cases the teacher may choose to give each group a named stream or, in the case of a large river, a section of the course of one river.

Ask each group to make a tracing of the river(s) and highlight on that tracing the main river features, such as meanders, small islands, waterfalls and drainage ditches. These features can either be labelled directly on the map or can be shown by symbols and a key. The children should make sure that all features relating to the river are mapped, including the effects of human activity such as building bridges or weirs or straightening rivers to improve drainage. Groups can then compare results. What are the commonest features on rivers? Which features create most problems for local people? Could these problems be overcome?

Follow-up
Ask the children to compare the local river with a larger European river such as the Rhine, the Danube or the Loire. What are the similarities? What are the differences?

Stream study

Age range
Nine to eleven.

Group size
Groups of four.

What you need
Photocopiable page 123, metre sticks, pens, pencils, measuring tapes, an orange for each group, wellingtons, plastic bags, ties, labels, a stop-watch per group. (Think about the number of adult supervisors needed and make sure everyone understands the need for safety.)

What to do
Explain to the children that they are going to carry out a geographical field survey of a stream. Stress safety points about behaviour in and around water. Each group should be allotted a site along the stream and will carry out the survey as detailed on the photocopiable pages.

Go through the photocopiable page 123 with the children so that they fully understand what they will be doing. In particular, stress the need for careful observation, especially in tasks 2–6. Similarly, explain the need for careful and accurate measurements in tasks 10 and 11. Task 12 may well highlight key points relating to pollution of the stream by cans or bottles, as well as how the stream changes along its course.

Tell the children to use the data collected to answer key questions such as:
● What colour is the water? How does this vary from point to point?
● How do the stream banks change?
● Does the water always flow at the same speed in streams? Where does it flow faster? Where does it flow more slowly?
● Is the stream the same depth all the way across? If not, how does the depth vary?
● Does the water flow fastest where the stream is deep or shallow?
● How does the material on the stream bed vary from point to point?
● Is the fine mud to be found in places where the stream is deep or shallow?
● Are the pebbles to be found where the stream is flowing fast or slowly?

Follow-up
Tell the groups to draw a cross-section of the stream at their survey point. They sould show how the depth varies, and how this affects the speed of water flow and the material to be found on the stream bed.

Links with other curriculum areas

English
- poetry and stories relating to water and water 'moods', e.g., storm and calm.

History
- water as a form of defence, and as a means across which attacks can be mounted.

Mathematics
- concepts of quantity and volume
- width;
- depth.

Water resources

Technology
- tackling ways to keep water out of the home;
- designing craft which will float;
- investigating bridge structure.

Science
- investigating:
- sinking and floating;
- freezing and melting;
- water and weather;
- water and power generation.

Music
- interpretation and representation of the sound and movement of water.

Art
- water patterns and colours;
- famous paintings of rivers and seas.

Mapping it out

Maps and mapping are basic to all geographical work. It is probably best to develop the skills involved in map reading in two contexts: (1) on their own to ensure that children have a clear grasp of ideas such as coordinates or plan view and (2) in the context of other geographical work such as studies of food, shops, soils, the park and so on. Many teachers use the first type of lesson as a separate, specific topic in which the skill is first learned. They then use the second type of lesson to enable children to practise and elaborate the skill. The second type of lesson also allows pupils to demonstrate their ability to transfer the skill learned to a variety of contexts. Hence the idea of plan view might initially be developed in relation to familiar objects such as toys and classroom furniture, then later elaborated in relation to a model of the local area, or a plan of a local park.

Because maps are so fundamental to so much geography, some teachers may feel intimidated by the technical vocabulary which has grown up around them such as a 1:1,250 map, or a six-figure grid reference. This can make for rather dull lessons which can become drill and practice. Map reading is not difficult (see Scholastic's *Starting geography: Mapping skills* (1993) by R. Bowles) and should above all be fun! The children should experience it as a series of games and fun activities with the emphasis on success. In this way the problem of early failure and disillusionment can be readily avoided.

Displays of a wide range of different maps around the classroom on a fairly constant basis will provide a reference point for all subsequent mapwork activities. Try to include lots of maps drawn by children, for example, routes to school, routes round a supermarket, a plan of a park, as well as published maps like the A–Z series and Ordnance Survey maps of the local area (1:50,000 and 1:1,250). The more children become used to seeing maps around them, the more easily they will accept them as a part of their everyday working life in many subject areas, not just geography.

Human geography
• features of the local environment such as roads, bridges, churches, railways
• local occupations

Physical geography
• local physical features such as hills, streams, rivers or coasts

Environmental geography
• local resources such as rivers, lakes, woodland, mines or rocks for quarrying

Themes

Skills

Places

Mapping it out

• mapwork skills – location, direction, use of compass, plan view, symbols, coordinates, using different kinds of map

• use of aerial photographs

• use of Ordnance Survey maps

• the local area
• the neighbourhood

Simon says

Age range
Five to seven.

Group size
Whole class.

What you need
A mobile or wall display showing words which describe location or direction. Such a list might include: above, below, behind, in front, backwards, on, off, next to, forwards, left, right, inside, outside, close, as well as the traditional directions of north, south, east and west.

What to do
Explain to the children that they are going to be using words which describe *where* things are, for example, the ruler is on the table, or the waste basket is behind the door.

Either the teacher or selected children can then give directions to specific members of the class such as Simon says Rashni should stand next to her desk, Joseph should go and stand close to the sink, Michelle should stand below the window and so on. In this way children will become familiar with using words which describe location, which is the basis of all maps.

Follow-up
Children can draw pictures to illustrate the meaning of each of the words, for example, showing themselves *close* to their home or *far* from their home, *on* their bicycle or *off* it.

Left and right

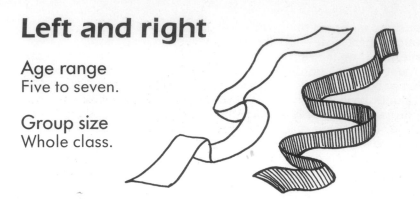

Age range
Five to seven.

Group size
Whole class.

What you need
Ribbons of two different colours (enough for two per child), paper, pencils and crayons.

What to do
Explain that the purpose of the game is to remember which is the child's right hand and which is the left. Give each child two different coloured ribbons and get them to tie one (for example red) to their left wrist and the other (for example green) to their right wrist.

Pick one child who is sitting at her table and ask her to name one item of furniture or one person who is to her left, and then one to her right. Practise this with three or four children in different parts of the classroom to demonstrate the importance of describing left and right in relation to each individual child. Then get each child to draw three things they can see to the right of them and three things they can see to the left of them. They should colour in each picture, for example, either red (to the left) or green (to the right), and write the words left and right at the top of their pictures.

Follow-up
Ask the children to list and draw four things that are to their left as they lie in bed, and four to their right.

Blindfold routes

Age range
Five to seven.

Group size
Whole class/groups of six or seven.

What you need
A scarf or material to make a blindfold.

What to do
Clear a space in the classroom of furniture and other hazards which a blindfolded child might fall over. Explain to the children that they are going to play a game in which one of them will be blindfolded and given directions to follow. Blindfold the chosen child then ask other children in turn to give directions for the blindfolded child to follow. These directions should include details of turning left, right or moving straight ahead or backwards, as well as the number of paces to be taken.

   The challenge is for the blindfolded child to follow each direction correctly. Let one blindfolded child follow about three or four directions before removing the blindfold and letting them see which part of the classroom they have ended up in. Then swap over and allow another child to be blindfolded. In this way children will become familiar with giving and following directions.

Follow-up
As the children become more adept at the game the instructions can be made more complex. Be careful that the blindfolded child does not become dizzy.

The view from above

Age range
Five to seven.

Group size
Whole class.

What you need
An overhead projector, toy vehicles, dolls house furniture, various coins, for example, 50p, one pound, 20p, 10p, paper, crayons and pencils.

What to do
Explain to the children that the aim of the game is to guess what each object is from its shape on the overhead projector. Explain that the light in the projector is shining straight down so we see only the view of each object from above.

Do not let the children see what you put on the projector. Start by placing some coins on the projector and let the children work out which is the 50p, 10p, 20p and so on. Why do they think it is difficult to distinguish between the 10p and the one pound coin? This should introduce the idea that we can use shapes as clues to work out what objects look like when seen from above.

Now put some toy vehicles on the projector and let the children work out which is which. How do the shapes help us (for example, aeroplanes have wings)? Which shapes can be confusing (for example, lorries and buses)?

Plan views

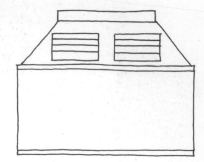

Age range
Five to seven.

Group size
Pairs.

What you need
Photocopiable page 124 for each pair, cut up into individual cards. (Photocopy on to card if possible).

What to do
Give each pair the side view and the plan view of the television set. Talk about the side view and what it shows. Encourage the children to talk about the plan view and say in what ways it is different, and how they know it is a television set.

Next, give each group a set of cards from photocopiable page 124 showing the side view of objects and a set of cards showing the plan view of the same objects. Ask the children to sort the cards into those views which are from above (plan view) and those which are taken from the side. They should then match up the plan view and the side view of each object.

Follow-up
The children could go on to draw their own pictures of plan view and side view of objects in the classroom, for example, books, a desk top, a globe, a satchel.

Compass directions

Age range
Five to nine.

Group size
Individuals.

What you need
Copies of photocopiable page 125 for each member of the class, paper fasteners, card, scissors, crayons, a compass, sugar paper.

What to do
Show the children a compass and talk about the main directions – north, south, east and west. Explain that the needle on a compass always points north then show them how to turn the compass until the point of the needle is directly positioned at the fixed north point on the compass. Tell them they are going to make a compass using photocopiable page 125. The children should cut out the compass shape, together with the pointer, then fix the pointer to the centre of each compass with a paper fastener.

   Now use a real compass to find out which is north, south, east and west in the classroom. Ask the children to align their compasses with the real compass so that everyone can see which is north, south and so on.

   Pin large labels on sheets of sugar paper and stick these on each wall of the classroom to identify the four main compass points. Now ask the children to write or draw pictures of things they can see to the south of the classroom, or to the east. What can they see to the north, or to the west?

Follow-up
Repeat the exercise at various points around the school. In each case the children should align their compasses with the real compass. This will reinforce the idea of directions and help in understanding how to use a compass.

Routes for the robot

Age range
Seven to nine.

Group size
Groups of four.

What you need
A programmable toy or robot such as Turtle, Big Trak
or Roamer, a computer and a computer program.

What to do
Explain to the children that the toy has been
programmed to follow directions and so can be made to
move forwards, backwards, sideways, left, right and so
on. Let them play with the equipment and get used to
seeing how the toy will move in relation to their
commands. Then get them to work out a route for the toy
to follow. This might involve the toy going left, right,
forwards and backwards to go around a chair, or along
a stretch of the classroom. Get the children to enter their
program in the computer and see if the toy does follow
their instructions.

Follow-up
As the children become more familiar with the toy and
with directions, get them to devise more complicated
routes for the toy to follow.

School plan

Age range
Seven to nine.

Group size
Pairs.

What you need
Copies of a large-scale plan of the school, paper, pencils, pens.

What to do
The aim of this activity is to make the children familiar with using plans of the school and understanding what plans do and do not show.

Give each pair of children a copy of the school plan. Talk about the plan and ask questions about what it shows, for example, where are the toilets shown on the plan? Where is the medical room shown on the plan? This is to ensure that the children fully understand the kind of things the plan shows.

Then give each pair of children a list of features (see below) to find on the plan. They should put a tick next to each feature if they can find it on the plan and a cross if they cannot. The types of features to look for on the plan include: front entrance, hall, television set, garden, telephone, radiator, office, headteacher's room, medical room, tables, sink, taps, drinking fountain, pegs, kitchen, classroom, toilets, computer and bookcase.

Now discuss the plan with the class. Which features were visible on the plan? Which were not? Why do the children think these were not shown on the plan? Ask them to consider if a large-scale plan of the classroom or other rooms shows some of the features not included on the whole-school plan.

Follow-up
Let groups draw a large-scale plan of the hall, or the medical room, or the office to show some features not included on the whole school plan. What features still cannot be included?

A new site for the school

Age range
Nine to eleven.

Group size
Groups of four.

What you need
Large-scale map of the local area – this could be an A–Z map or an Ordnance Survey 1:2,500 or 1:25,000.

What to do
Tell the children to imagine that their school has to move to a new site. The aim is to try and find a new site as close as possible to the existing one but which has more space and more advantages, such as being central to bus routes or being situated away from a dangerous main road.

Divide the class into groups. Each group has to study the large-scale maps of the area and investigate different sites. Eventually each group should select one site which they think would be the best one to move to. Make sure each group has a different site.

Each group now has to prepare a short report on its proposed new site. The reports should include:
- a sketch map of the site to show its size, layout and surrounding land use, for example, railway line, factories, houses, parkland;
- a series of reasons why they feel this would make the best new site, including what advantages it has over the existing site.

Each group should then present its report on the chosen site and the other groups can ask questions and make observations. At the end the children abandon their group roles and take a class vote on which would be the most popular site.

Follow-up
The groups could each design the layout for a new school on the chosen site, showing on their maps how they have solved any problems of the existing site and buildings, such as the creation of a new wildlife area, or building a larger hall.

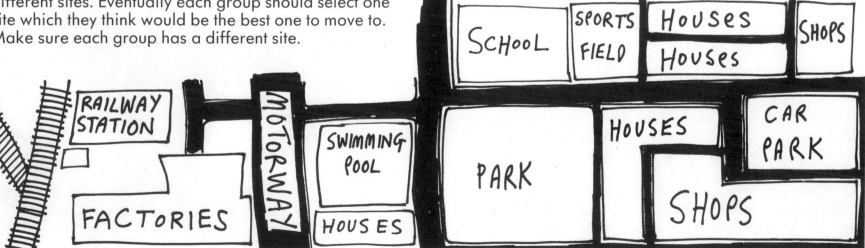

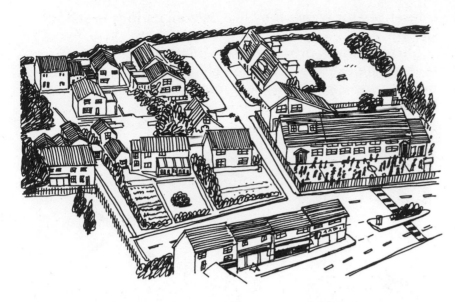

Studying aerial photographs

Age range
Nine to eleven.

Group size
Groups of four or six.

What you need
Copies of an oblique aerial photograph of the school and its surrounding area, numbered dots, a large-scale map (A–Z or Ordnance Survey 1:1,250 or 1:10,000) of the area covered by the aerial photograph; paper, pens.

What to do
Put a series of numbered dots at key points on the air photograph to show features such as roads, railway lines, houses (different types), school, shops, offices and so on.

Explain to the group that you want them to identify as many features as possible shown on the aerial photograph. The children have to list the numbers and, alongside each, name the feature shown. They should also compare the aerial photograph with the large-scale map of the area, and use the map to identify and name some of the numbered features for example St Giles' Church, the bus station, a detached house in Burton Crescent.

Follow-up
Repeat the exercise but this time use a vertical aerial photograph of the same area. Can the children still identify the features even though they look different in this photograph? Which features are easy to identify? Which are difficult?

Using a 1:50,000 Ordnance Survey map

Age range
Nine to eleven.

Group size
Pairs.

What you need
Copies of the Ordnance Survey 1:50,000 (Landranger) map which shows the school and part of the surrounding area – select an area about 15cm square; paper, pens.

What to do
The aim of this activity is to help children become confident in using 1:50,000 Ordnance Survey maps. Give each pair of children an extract (15cm x 15cm) of the local 1:50,000 Ordnance Survey map. Talk to them about some of the features that the map shows, for example, main roads in red, motorways in blue. Ask the children to identify some of the features shown on the map, such as B class roads and minor roads, rivers and streams, schools, woodland, canals, lakes, cemeteries, colleges and sites of ancient monuments.

Next, ask the children to give four-figure grid references for each of the features that they identify. Explain that in a four-figure reference, the first two figures given are the *eastings* (the horizontal lines running left to right on a map), for example 51, and the second two figures are *northings* (the vertical lines running top to bottom on a map), for example, 05 – giving a reference of 5105. The rest of the class can then check the grid reference and check the symbol or point of interest. Then ask the children to give four-figure grid references for where they live as well as for the school site.

Once children are able to do this with confidence reverse the exercise. Give the children grid references and ask them to identify features in the squares you have specified.

Follow-up
Ask the children to describe what they would see to their right and to their left in the correct order if they were walking along a specified 2km stretch of road or footpath.

Links with other curriculum areas

PE
- orienteering.

English
- stories and poems about journeys using maps such as *Treasure Island*.

Mathematics
- measurements of distance and scale;
- coordinates;
- bearings.

History
- voyages of discovery and the use of maps over time to locate places;
- changing views of the map of the world pre- and post-Columbus.

Mapping it out

Technology
- taking photographs of objects and places from both side and oblique angles to compare the two, then taking a vertical photograph to show plan view.

Science
- features of the local area, such as rocks, woodland, rivers, and their properties.

Art
- different styles of map, including styles of symbol used on different scales;
- ways of portraying features on small-scale maps.

Food and farming

These topics can provide the basis for many geographical projects which start from a direct link with the children's own experiences. All children need and consume a great variety of different foods and all have their own preferences and prejudices. Consequently, this interest provides a good starting point for considering where food originates and how it arrives in shops and supermarkets. The main aim is to open children's eyes to the different sources from which food is produced, for example, milk from cows and bread from wheat. The intention is to help children to look beyond food as pre-packaged, weighed, sliced, wrapped and processed, and begin to look at what is happening *before* it becomes a supermarket product. There is an earlier stage at which someone *produces* the food. This is the important link between food consumers and food producers, between food and farming.

Food and farming are also ideal topics for introducing or developing ideas about the wider world. Many children do not realise just how far some food travels to reach their homes, for example, bananas from the West Indies or butter from New Zealand. In this context the aim is to use food as an introduction to the study of life in these more distant places. It is also important to consider the idea of our interdependence with people in other parts of the world, who supply us with food and whom, in return, we supply with other goods such as oil or manufactured goods.

Many children will have little experience of the countryside (except through leisure activities) and even less of farms. Hence, for children in urban areas a visit to a farm is a vital part of the range of experiences they will need to function as effective citizens in later life. Young children need to experience the thrill of stroking a chicken or a cow or the excitement of collecting eggs to deepen and enlarge their understanding of both food and farming. Older children need to see how farming is big business, using computerised weather forecasts and the most up-to-date equipment in order to produce as much food as cost-efficiently as possible. Only in this way will they develop a respect and understanding for the work of farmers in Britain and other countries.

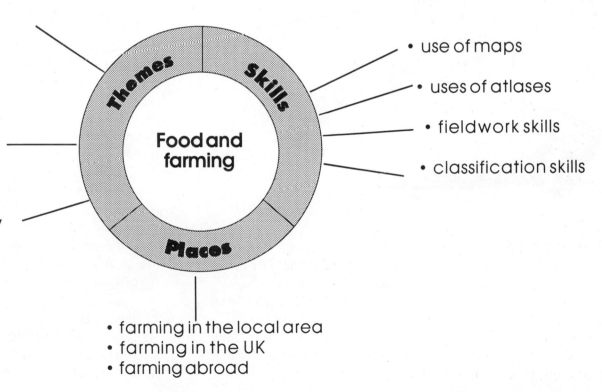

Human geography
• people and food
• people and farming
• farming and transport
• farms and farming

Physical geography
• farming and weather
• farming and the landscape

Environmental geography
• farming and the environment

Themes | Skills

Places

Food and farming

• use of maps
• uses of atlases
• fieldwork skills
• classification skills

• farming in the local area
• farming in the UK
• farming abroad

Labels

Age range
Five to seven.

Group size
Pairs.

What you need
A range of food items from a shop or supermarket such as a jar of coffee, a box of tea bags, a box of cakes, a packet of biscuits, a loaf of bread, a tub of margarine, a box of eggs, a pot of yoghurt, a piece of cheese. In all cases remove the label from the product. A set of labels from other foods, for example, meat, bread, tins of fish, tins of fruit, paper, crayons, paints.

What to do
Give a label to each pair of children. Encourage the children to talk about the nature of the information on their product labels, for example, the brand name of the product, what it contains — tea, coffee, bread and so on and how much it contains. Let the children discuss other features of the label such as diagrams, pictures or photographs. Do the labels show what is inside the packet? What else do they show (for example, people picking the product)? How do the labels use colour? What colours are used? Which colours do the children notice first?

Explain to the children that each pair will be given a product such as a jar, a tin, a packet or a pot. Their task is to design a label for this product which will be attractive when people see it on the supermarket shelf.

At the end of the activity display the labels alongside the products and discuss each label with the class. Hold a vote on which is the most effective label.

Follow-up
Ask the children to look at other information on labels, such as instructions for use, sell-by dates and bar codes and talk about the importance of each.

Packaging

Age range
Five to seven.

Group size
Group of six.

What you need
A small amount of different foods such as bread, sugar, tea leaves, coffee beans, honey, yoghurt, milk and margarine each on a separate saucer; a bag of crisps in its packet and a bottle of soft drink. A selection of plastic bags, paper bags and empty containers, e.g. bottles, jars, tubs and boxes.

What to do
Talk to the children about the fact that most food and drink comes in some type of packaging, for example a bag of crisps in a sealed foil packet to keep the contents fresh. Discuss the idea that different types of food need different types of packaging. For example, liquids are usually packaged in bottles (glass or plastic) or tins. Talk about why this is the case (to avoid losing contents and to make it easy to stack containers on top of each other).

Discuss the different types of lids on containers, for example ring pulls, plastic seals and twist tops. Talk about how easy or difficult it is to get into some food packaging. Let the children suggest why some foods need special types of top, for example, airtight air seal (to make the contents last longer).

Give each pair of children a small amount of a food on a saucer, such as sugar, tea leaves, coffee beans, honey, milk, jam, yoghurt, bread and margarine. Ask them to experiment with different types of packaging such as plastic bags, paper bags, bottles, tubs and jars and decide which suits their food best. The children should then draw a picture of their food in its container. At the end of the activity they should match up the foods with the original containers. Which foods can be packed in lots of different containers?

A model farm

Age range
Five to seven.

Group size
Groups of four.

What you need
A model layout of a farm (to include fences, barns, machinery such as tractors, combine harvesters, land rovers, sprayers and so on, animals such as pigs, sheep, hens, cattle, dogs, cats, people, fruit trees), pictures of barley, wheat, maize and other crops growing in the fields, packets of wheat flakes, fresh corn on the cob.

What to do
Let the children play with the model of the farm. Talk to them about the different parts of the farm. The aim is to help them to recognise that farms are made up of *fields*, in which crops grow, *animals* which are reared in fields or barns, and *buildings* such as the farmhouse and the machinery sheds, as well as *people* and *pets*. Encourage them to talk about the different machines used on the farm and the type of work each does, for example, tractors for pulling the plough or for moving bales of straw and combine harvesters for harvesting wheat or barley.

Talk about the different foods produced on farms, such as milk, vegetables, eggs, meat and fruit. Show the children the pictures of cereals such as wheat, barley and maize. Talk about how the seeds are planted in the fields, how the plants grow and are then harvested. Show them some cereal foods such as wheat flakes or corn on the cob and ask them to draw a simple flow chart showing the journey of the cereal from the field to the finished product in the supermarket. They can illustrate each stage if they like.

Follow-up
Talk about the journey of milk from cow to supermarket or doorstep and ask the children to outline, in the same way, the stages of milk production from cow to doorstep.

Food changes

Age range
Five to nine.

Group size
Whole class.

What you need
Different types of food, e.g. a banana, a slice of bread, a carrot, a piece of cake, a pepper, a mushroom, an egg, a piece of lettuce, a tomato.

What to do
Talk to the children about how food changes over time. For instance, some foods dry out while others, such as milk, go sour. Display a selection of different foods in the classroom. Tell the children that they are to study the foods and predict how they will change during the course of a week.

Then each day for a week the children should record how each food changes in terms of colour, shape, size and smell and note any other features of change that occur. How accurate were their predictions? Which food changed most? Which changed least?

Next, ask the children to consider how the foods could have been made to last longer. For example, bread turned into toast will last longer. Storing foods in a fridge or freezer will make them last longer. Putting some foods, such as mushrooms, into cans makes them last longer.

Follow-up
Repeat the activity but this time bury the foods in a large plant pot in the classroom filled with sand. Do the foods last longer when buried in the ground?

Farm visit

Age range
Five to eleven.

Group size
Whole class.

What you need
Clipboards, a copy of the farm questionnaire on photocopiable page 126, copies of the farm layout, pens, pencils.

What to do
Arrange to visit a farm. The Association of Agriculture has a Farm Study Scheme which will put you in touch with a local farm willing to take pupils. Their address can be found in the Resources section on page 128. Make a preliminary visit to the farm to get a map of its layout and an idea of what you want the children to see and do.

Give each child a copy of the farm layout and questionnaire and explain that they will be visiting this farm and will be able to ask the farmer some questions. Talk about the things that take place on the farm such as milking, ploughing, harvesting and ask the children to add their own questions to the photocopiable sheet. Tell them that as they go around the farm, they will be labelling the fields they see on their layout plans with the crops growing in them and noting down building use. The farmer will be able to help the children complete their questionnaires.

It is essential that the children understand that farms, with all their machinery and animals, can be dangerous places. Hence, attention to safety and sensible behaviour is important at all times during their visit.

Follow-up
Tell the children to draw pictures and write about the farm, with particular reference to:
● how the land is used, for example, what crops are grown and how this changes from year to year;
● what the crops are used for, for example, feeding to animals, sold for flour milling;
● what animals are reared, and what is produced from them;
● what machinery is used, at what time of year and for what purpose;
● what chemicals are used, and for what purpose;
● the number of workers on the farm, and how this changes throughout the year.

Ask the children to make a wall display of their descriptions of the farm, together with an enlarged layout map of the farm showing land use. A model of the layout showing use of the farm buildings would be another useful addition to the display and could be positioned on a table beneath.

Farming abroad

Age range
Five to eleven.

Group size
Whole class.

What you need
A case study of a farm in an economically developing country (see Resources section for details) to include a map of the farm, details of the farmer's day, details of crops grown, animals kept, local weather and climate, local markets, workers on the farm, housing on the farm and machinery used (a video of the farm and/or photographs are important elements of this study); sugar paper, paints, pens, empty cereal boxes.

What to do
If working with younger children, ask them to draw pictures to show the work being done on the farm at different times of the day and at different times of the year. The pictures, together with brief descriptions should include the crops grown, animals kept, machinery used and local housing. Models of the houses on the farm or in the village in which most people live can be made from old cereal and other boxes.

Ask older children to write a play based on a typical day on a farm in an economically developing country. The play should include details of what people wear, how they are affected by the weather, and what they like or dislike about living on a farm, as well as the work they each do during the day. The play could be centred around a particular farming event, for example, harvest.

Follow-up
Let the children perform their play to another class. What do these children think about the advantages and disadvantages of living on a farm in an economically developing country?

Different types of farming

Age range
Nine to eleven.

Group size
Whole class working in two groups.

What you need
Pictures, maps, video and written details of two different types of farm, for instance, a hill sheep farm and a mixed farm or an arable farm, for instance, a hill sheep farm and mixed farm or an arable farm (these case studies can be obtained from the Association of Agriculture – see Resources section for address); paper, pens, sugar paper.

What to do
Give each group the information for one type of farm. Explain that they have to produce a display about their farm to answer the following key questions:
1. Where is the farm? (A map should show its location in relation to nearby towns and main roads.)
2. What are the fields used for? (This would require a farm layout map plus explanation of what crops are grown.)
3. What are the main soil types? (This should be marked on the map.)
4. What is the main source of income on the farm? (For example, sale of animals, sale of milk.)
5. What is the size of the farm? (This should be shown on the layout map.)
6. What is the climate of the area around the farm? (The children would have to draw climate graphs.)
7. What machinery is used on the farm?

8. What are the main types of work in winter? (For example, ploughing, feeding animals and so on – this would be best represented in a pie graph.)
9. What are the main types of work in summer? (For example, spraying crops, shearing sheep – best represented in a pie graph.)
10. What type of field boundries are there on the farm? (For example, hedges, stone walls, metal fences – these should be shown on the map.)
11. How have government and EC (European Community) regulations affected the farm?

Once the two wall displays are complete the children should compare the farms using the eleven key questions. What are the main differences? What are the similarities? What are the reasons for the differences? (Possibilities include climate, location, aspect and soils.) Ask the children to write explanations for as many of the contrasts as possible.

Follow-up
Ask each group to choose one of the farms and compare it, using the same key questions, with a farm in a European country, such as France, or an economically developing country, such as India.

Links with other curriculum areas

Mathematics
- classification, sorting, measuring.

English
- poems and stories about food, its importance to people and the dangers of too much or too little.
- farming and the countryside in poetry and fiction.

Technology
- designing and making different types of labels and bar codes and different types of containers for a range of foods, e.g. frozen, liquid, solid, granular;
- how farm machinery works.

Food and farming

Art
- work connected with designing and making posters or short video commercials to promote particular food products. What are the key promotional points?
- rural and farming scenes in painting.

Science
- properties of foods and how foods decay and change over time;
- new farming techniques;
- developments in third world agriculture.

History
- importance of food as a spur to voyages of discovery – search for new sources of food and new types of food, e.g. spice trade;
- farming developments.

Time off

Leisure is a popular theme with both children and teachers. It is associated with the enjoyment and pleasure of holidays and extra-curricular activities and may be the source of happy memories. Many schools approach leisure topics in the summer term, prior to visits made by classes or by children themselves during July and August. However there is much to be said for studying this theme in the spring term, when parents and children are planning for the coming summer. There is a ready supply of brochures, posters and other publicity material at this time, and it can be used to give that edge of reality to discussions, for example, just how far is it from London to Inverness, or from Birmingham to Miami?

Approaches which focus on local leisure facilities are just as valid as those looking at more exotic locations. The range, scale, location and use of local leisure facilities are important aspects of any community. They are frequently the cause of dispute when cuts in their numbers or size are proposed. There may well be an important local issue to be investigated here and the attitude of the local council towards leisure provision for children can be particularly interesting and relevant.

Human geography
- how different individuals use their leisure time
- leisure facilities in urban and rural areas
- travelling for leisure
- people who work in the leisure industry

Physical geography
- the use of different landscapes for leisure, from rivers to mountains and caves

Environmental geography
- the impact of leisure on the environment, e.g., footpath erosion
- location of leisure areas such as National Parks

Time off

Themes

Skills

Places

- use of maps on a variety of scales, including Ordnance Survey maps

- use of photographs

- use of tape recorders, video equipment in conducting interviews or surveys

- fieldwork skills including mapping and interviewing

- time off in the local area
- contrast with time off activity in another locality

Our park

Age range
Five to seven.

Group size
Whole class.

What you need
Photographs of scenes in parks (such as swings, roundabouts, fast food kiosks, tennis courts, bowling greens, flower beds, ponds, people jogging, people with dogs and so on); art materials, paper, pens.

What to do
The aim of this activity is to get children to think about the uses of a park, i.e., for leisure but also for work. It is also to get them to think about key *places* in the park. Ask the children about their visits to a park in summer. Which park do they go to? What things are in the park (for example, swings, trees, pond, stream, football pitches)? What do the children enjoy most about visits to the park? What do adults do who visit the park (for example, walk the dog, jogging)? Can they get things to eat and drink in the park? How often do they visit the park?

Arrange for a local park-keeper to visit the school and ask the children to compile a series of questions they would like him to answer. Perhaps he could give a talk with slides and photographs. Ask the park-keeper to describe his favourite place in the park and explain why he likes it so much.

Ask the children, with the help of the park-keeper, to describe some of the *jobs* people do in the park, such as weeding, mowing the grass, marking out playing fields, collecting litter and selling food and drinks.

Follow-up
Ask the children to draw a scene in the park in winter to highlight the differences in trees, clothing, activities, and so on.

Holiday

Age range
Five to seven.

Group size
Whole class.

What you need
Travel posters for UK resorts or National Parks, leaflets and brochures of holiday destinations in the UK, art materials, paper.

What to do
Ask the children to think about going on holiday in Britain for a few days or a week. They should consider the types of places they could visit, for example seaside holiday resorts like Blackpool, mountain or hill areas like Snowdon, lakes like Windermere, historic towns like York, coasts with very few towns, like Cornwall.

Then carry out a class survey of the types of places the children would most like to visit. They can then draw a simple picture graph of the results.

Now ask the children to draw a picture of the place they would most like to visit, then list the attractions such as lakes, seaside or mountains. Then ask them to write a paragraph promoting their chosen place to tourists. They should refer to the holiday brochures for tips on style and content. When they have finished, the children can mount their pictures together with their paragraph to make a pamphlet. They can then design a cover with a slogan advertising their chosen place. The pamphlets can be used in role-play activities about a visit to the travel agents.

Distances to the coast

Age range
Seven to eleven.

Group size
Whole class.

What you need
Copies of photocopiable page 115, an atlas between each two pupils, rulers.

What to do
Explain to the children that they are going to investigate different places on the coast and find out the distances between them and their own town or village. Give each child a copy of photocopiable page 115 and get them to use an atlas to name these towns: Penzance, Newquay, Torquay, Weymouth, Portsmouth, Brighton, Eastbourne, Dover, Margate, Southend, Great Yarmouth, Grimsby, Hull, Bridlington, Scarborough, Whitby, Whitley Bay, Edinburgh, Dundee, Inverness, Oban, Ayr, Stranraer, Blackpool, Llandudno, Barmouth, Aberystwyth, Weston-super-Mare, Minehead, Ilfracombe and Bude.

Now ask them to mark and name their own town or village with a dot. Then let the children measure straight line distances between their local town and each coastal town. Which is the nearest? Which is furthest away?

Now tell the children to add the main motorways to their map. They should label each one, then say which one(s) they would use on a journey from their local town to each seaside settlement. Which motorways would receive most use? What possible problems could arise from this heavy use? How could these problems be alleviated?

Follow-up
The children could mark non-coastal holiday towns on their map and measure distances to places like York, Windermere, Buxton and Bath. This will highlight the importance of non-coastal places for leisure and the different attractions of these places.

Using and abusing the park

Age range
Seven to eleven.

Group size
Pairs.

What you need
Paper, pens, art materials, photocopiable page 127.

What to do
Give a copy of photocopiable page 127 to each pair of children and explain that it shows a park in a large town. In their pairs ask them to examine the picture to identify all the things that people are doing wrong in the scene. They can list these then draw speech bubbles to show what the people nearby might be saying. For example, the woman seated on the bench might be saying to her companion, 'Look at that man dropping litter on the grass.'

Let each pair of children read out their list and speech bubbles and let everyone discuss the results. Is everyone in agreement as to what would be said? Then each pair should make another list of ways in which they could improve the park to stop people abusing it, for example, by putting more litter bins in the park, especially close to fast food or drink outlets, sectioning off some parts of the park for games and others for just sitting quietly.

Follow-up
Ask the children to design eye-catching signs to go in the park to stop people abusing it, such as a boot above a flower with the words 'Do not trample the flowers' below.

Leisure diary

Age range
Seven to eleven.

Group size
Whole class.

What you need
A database, pens, paper.

What to do
Explain to the children that they are going to keep a leisure diary for the next week. They should record what they do in their leisure time each day using a table like the one shown opposite. The record should show the activity involved, such as visiting a friend to play a computer game, watching television, going swimming, going to a disco, riding a bicycle, playing a sport. The diary should also show how long is spent on each activity.

At the end of the week, enter the information from the whole class on a database. Older children could enter the data themselves. The aim is to help the children to record details other than each kind of activity, such as where it took place, who was involved, how long it lasted and so on. Then tell the children to interrogate the data to answer such questions as:
- What was the most popular leisure activity?
- Which leisure activity took the longest time?
- Do girls enjoy the same leisure activities as boys?
- What was the least popular activity?
- Which person had most leisure time?
- Which person had least leisure time?
- Which activities were in the home?
- Which activities were in places other than the home?
- Which activities were outdoor?

Follow-up
Ask another class in the school of a different age to complete a similar survey and then help the children to compare results.

DAY	MORNING	AFTERNOON	EVENING
MON			T.V. – 1½ hrs Play –1 hr
TUES			
WED		SWIMMING –1hr	
THUR			
FRI			
SAT			
SUN	Ride Bike–1hr		

Holidays at home and abroad

Age range
Seven to eleven.

Group size
Groups of three.

What you need
Holiday brochures for destinations all over the world, large map of Britain, large world map a database, coloured dots.

What to do
Get the children to carry out a class survey of holiday destinations for the previous year. Teachers will need to be sensitive to the needs of individuals and groups who may not have had a holiday. The teacher could ask them to list places they have visited in the past or places they would like to visit. Let the children enter the information on a database and then interrogate it, to discover which were the most popular holiday destinations. Were they in England, Wales or Scotland? Were they abroad? Mark these destinations on a map of Britain and the world.

  Next, divide the children into groups and give each group some holiday brochures. Tell the groups to select a particular place in one country that they would like to visit. The children should analyse the information in the brochure about their chosen place under the headings:
- natural attractions of the place, for example, sunshine, cliffs, caves, sea, rain forest;
- facilities provided, for example, hotels, restaurants, discos, safari tours;
- local customs, for example, food, dance, dress;

- other attractions, for example, places of historic interest such as temples or castles.

  Each group should then give a report to the rest of the class explaining the location of their chosen place, its attractions and what can be seen and done on a visit there. Younger children could draw pictures and provide simple descriptions of activities. Older children could draw up a diary for a week's activities including visits to local attractions. They could then justify their choice and link the results with the original class survey of holiday destinations.

Follow-up
Encourage the groups to become experts in a particular foreign holiday place, such as Spain, Italy, the Caribbean and set themselves up as travel agents to supply information to parents, teachers or other classes about holidays in other countries.

Local leisure

Age range
Seven to eleven.

Group size
Pairs or groups of three.

What you need
Large-scale map of the town, Yellow Pages or local trade directories, a map of local bus routes, paper, pens.

What to do
Ask the children to list as many types of local leisure facility as possible, including bingo halls, cinemas, swimming baths, leisure centres, discos, ice rinks and so on. Refer to Yellow Pages and trade directories for any other leisure facilities in other parts of the town and add their names and addresses to the list.

Allocate an area of the town to each group. On a large-scale map of the area, each group should plot the location of each leisure facility. The groups should then try to explain the pattern of facilities in their area. For example, are they all on main roads? Are they all on bus routes? Are they all close to car parks? Are they close to shopping centres?

Each group should then produce a map with coloured dots showing the distribution of facilities. These maps should fit together like a jigsaw to reveal the whole town. Beside each area mount the explanation of the patterns shown.

Follow-up
Ask the children to survey parents, friends, relatives and other pupils, listing the leisure facilities they use in the town and those new ones they would like to see provided. Then encourage the class to consider the best location for the new facilities.

Planning a leisure facility

Age range
Nine to eleven.

Group size
Pairs.

What you need
Details of a proposed leisure facility to include a swimming pool, gym, sauna, toilets, badminton courts, squash courts, table tennis areas, dance areas, changing rooms with showers, as well as a restaurant area and car parking with access throughout for disabled people; A3 sheets of paper, art materials.

What to do
Explain to the children that they have been given the task of designing a new leisure centre. They have to include all the facilities on the proposal. They must locate these elements within one building and explain the reasons behind the layout they design. For example, they may choose to have the café as a central area where people can meet and locate the toilets nearby. They must always keep in mind the needs of the disabled and safety aspects.

Ask each pair to map out their design for the leisure centre, then shade and label each of the activity areas such as the swimming pool, squash courts and so on. They should write a brief explanation of the layout which should be used when each pair presents their design to the rest of the class.

Follow-up
Ask the manager/ess of a local leisure centre to visit the school and comment on the children's designs particularly from the point of access for disabled people.

LEISURE CENTRE: GROUND FLOOR

Theme park on our doorstep

Age range
Nine to eleven.

Group size
Groups of four.

What you need
Brochures of theme parks and their attractions.

What to do
Explain to the children that they have to imagine that a theme park, which includes wild animals as well as a wide range of rides, is to be built on the site of the local park. Give each group a role which they have to develop as an argument either for or against the new theme park. They have to decide what the people they represent might think about the proposal and then list the points those people would make at a planning enquiry either for or against the project. The main groups could be:
• residents whose houses would be close to the park and who are worried about escaped animals;
• people worried about traffic jams as visitors flock to the park;
• people keen to visit the attraction and try the rides;
• people who hope to get a job in the new theme park;
• people who want to keep the existing park;
• people who want to see the site developed as a wildlife area;
• people such as café owners or garage owners who would make money from visitors to the park.

Once each group has developed its ideas, ask the children to elect a chairperson to run a planning enquiry

into whether the project should go ahead or not. Let each group present its ideas and arguments. Then other groups can challenge them or ask questions. At the end let the children abandon their roles and vote for or against the proposed theme park.

Links with other curriculum areas

Mathematics
- different leisure activities of different groups, work on:
  – sorting;
  – sets;
  – graphs.

Technology
- designing and making different types of equipment suitable for leisure activities, from kites to water-resistant types of footwear.

History
- how use of leisure time has changed through time;
- different types of leisure pursuits and their evolution.

Time off

Science
- Exploring the properties of materials involved in time-off activities, e.g.: heat resistance; insulation; durability.

English
- poems and stories about leisure and its link with work;
- people's attitudes to leisure – personal accounts.

Art
- pictures and models based on the different settings for leisure time – the countryside, rivers and lakes, the seaside or urban areas.

Natural resources, pollution and conservation

The Geography National Curriculum pays particular attention to the environment, especially its use and abuse, through Attainment Target 5, Environmental geography. This states that 'Pupils should demonstrate their increasing knowledge and understanding of:

1. the use and misuse of natural resources;
2. the quality and vulnerability of different environments; and
3. the possibilities for protecting and managing environments.'

Within this context there is great scope for teachers to encourage their pupils to consider environmental issues related to the use of resources as well as pollution and conservation. As with most projects, those relating to natural resources, pollution and conservation need to be firmly based within the child's own experience. Hence small-scale, local examples of resources, such as people involved in extracting resources, may well form the basis of early investigations. Later, larger-scale examples such as coal mining and fishing or even the development of Antarctica's resources can be addressed once the children have grasped some basic ideas about resources.

There is a similar progression in terms of scale and location for conservation issues. Small-scale local conservation issues should form the basis of early studies. Issues such as improvements to the school grounds or the establishment of a wildlife area are suitable types of project for pupils of all ages. Later, more distant, larger-scale conservation issues, such as the work of National Parks in Britain and abroad, may well form the basis of geography projects.

By their very nature, projects on resources, pollution and conservation will raise issues related to values and attitudes. Teachers need not fear such issues, but should be aware that in the examination of projects, such as the development of Antarctica's resources or the construction of a local bypass, there will always be groups of people in favour of the proposal and others against it. The teacher's role will be to classify the views held by different groups involved in such projects and confirm that there may be no one 'right' answer in the conflict over an issue. Rather, pupils need to be helped to realise that virtually all projects have an environmental impact, which has to be researched and assessed before any judgements can be made as to the merits of the project.

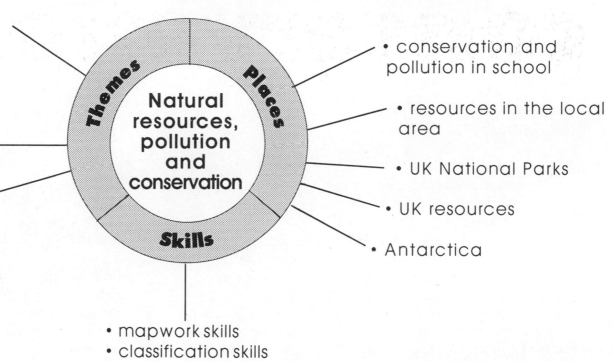

Human geography
- people and resources
- industry, resources and pollution
- jobs and resources

Physical geography
- plants, animals, insects

Environmental geography
- different types of resources
- different environments and their vulnerability
- pollution and conservation of resources

Themes

Natural resources, pollution and conservation

Places
- conservation and pollution in school
- resources in the local area
- UK National Parks
- UK resources
- Antarctica

Skills
- mapwork skills
- classification skills

Resources

Age range
Five to seven.

Group size
Whole class working in four groups.

What you need
Pictures of: items made of wood, e.g. furniture, pencils, window frames; items made from materials quarried out of the ground, e.g. slate, limestone, a gemstone in a ring, coal; items which come from the sea such as different types of fish, corals and shells; items which come from animals such as wool, milk and eggs; large sheets of paper, pens, paint and brushes.

What to do
Show the children the pictures of the different items, for example, fish, wool, milk, roofing slates and furniture. In each case talk about what each item is and what it is used for, but stress where it comes from, for example, from the sea, from trees, from animals or from under the ground. Divide the wall display area into these four groups and give each one a heading. Ask the children to draw pictures of other items which come from each of the four categories. Then tell them to sort their own pictures and those used in the introduction into the correct groups, label them and stick these on the wall display.

Follow-up
Add some specific examples of each of the four categories to the wall display such as sea shells, pieces of slate or marble, milk cartons and cardboard shoe boxes.

Jobs and resources

Age range
Five to seven.

Group size
Groups of four.

What you need
Pictures and general information on fishing, mining, quarrying and lumbering. If possible, the information should include an example of a person who is involved in each activity, together with details of what they do and why it is important. Other items to include are pictures of the types of equipment used by each group, such as chain saws, coal-cutting equipment, fishing nets and so on. If possible, arrange for a person who has experience of working in one or more of these occupations to come and talk to the children.

What to do
Give each group information and pictures about one of the activities. Ask them to produce a folder of pictures, stories and general information about the work of their activity. Stress the importance of showing in their pictures the ways in which the activity affects the environment, for example, cutting down trees, digging away quarries in a hillside, digging coal from underground or catching fish in the ocean.

Each group should then present their folder to the rest of the class and talk briefly about the work of the people and why their work is so important, for example, providing us with wood, fish, stone, coal and so on.

Follow-up
Select one of the activities such as fishing or lumbering and then arrange a visit to a local museum to study how the methods used have changed in the last fifty years and what steps have been taken to reduce the dangers of the job.

Improving the school grounds

Age range
Five to eleven.

Group size
Whole class.

What you need
Wild flower seeds, old wooden logs, a bird table and bird food including peanuts; flower pots, stones, old bricks, a dustbin lid, trowels and rakes; reference books for bird, insect and minibeast identification.

What to do
Talk to the children about the different types of wildlife they can see around the school grounds. Ask them to carry out a survey of the number and types of wild bird seen from the classroom during the course of a week. They should record their results.

Take the children on a search for minibeasts in the school grounds and again record the number, type and location of beasts found. They could also carry out a survey of the number, type and location of insects seen from the classroom window during a week in spring or summer.

Next, discuss with the children what could be done to make the school grounds more attractive to wildlife. For example, setting up a bird table with food within sight of the classroom might increase the number and variety of birds visiting the area. Talk about how butterflies, bees and other insects are attracted by certain types of bush and flower such as wild flowers and buddleia. Ask the children to suggest where these might be planted to attract more insects and, if funds and governors permit, plant an area with wild flowers and/or bushes.

Ask the children to suggest sites around the school where old logs, stones, bricks and empty flower pots might be located to increase the numbers of visiting minibeasts. An upturned dustbin lid is also a good magnet for attracting minibeasts.

Next, repeat the surveys of birds, insects and minibeasts after the changes have been implemented for a month or so. The surveys may cover a week or even a month in some cases. How have the number, range and location of birds, insects and minibeasts changed? Has the project benefited wildlife?

Follow-up
Use photographs, drawings, paintings, pictures and maps to produce a wall display showing how the school has become a friendlier place for wildlife.

Likes and dislikes in the local environment

Age range
Seven to eleven.

Group size
Whole class.

What you need
Pencils, clip boards.

What to do
Explain to the children that they will be going on a short walk around the area close to the school. The aim of the walk is to identify characteristics of different places within that environment. The children will be asked to describe their feelings about the places. The aim is not that every child should agree on what is a nice place or a noisy place, but rather that they look critically at the elements that make up their immediate environment.

As the children walk around the route they should select particular places such as bus stops, busy road junctions or parks, and write the names of these places in the appropriate sections on a table like the one opposite which correspond to their feelings about them. The teacher may choose to stop at particular places that children might ignore, such as litter bins or car parks or advertisement billboards, and ask children to think about these places as well as the more obvious ones.

Back in the classroom ask the children to draw pictures and write about the different types of places that they have seen – busy, quiet, pleasant, dangerous and so on.

Follow-up
For some of the places that the children have said they dislike, ask them to suggest ways in which they could be improved, such as collecting litter, emptying bins more frequently or installing railings to prevent danger.

PLACES AROUND SCHOOL

THIS PLACE(S) IS QUIET	
THIS PLACE(S) IS NOISY	
THIS PLACE(S) IS DANGEROUS	
THIS PLACE(S) IS PRETTY	
THIS PLACE(S) DOES NOT SMELL NICE	
THIS PLACE(S) IS BUSY	

I LIKE _ _ _ _ _ _ _ _ _ _ _ _ BECAUSE
(name of place)

I DISLIKE _ _ _ _ _ _ _ _ _ _ BECAUSE
(name of place)

Which class generates most litter?

Age range
Seven to eleven.

Group size
Pairs or groups of four.

What you need
Litter bins collected from the other classrooms of the school at the end of the working day, labelled and retained for study the following day; plastic bags, plastic or rubber gloves, card, pens, a database.

What to do
Explain to the class that they are going to study how much litter and other waste each class produces at the end of one working day. Arrange for groups of pupils to collect the full litter bins from each classroom at the end of a day and label each bin with the appropriate class number. Then, wearing rubber or plastic gloves, the children should:
● weigh the litter produced by each class and record the results;
● sort the litter from each class into categories such as waste school paper, paper wrappers and paper bags, plastic items, cans and bottles, old pencils or pens, food items and other materials. Then they should record the number of items in each category for each class.

● suggest which items from the waste bins could be recycled, for instance paper and aluminium cans.
   Present the results as a display, showing the amount and type of waste generated by each class, and how this varies in its amount, volume, composition and capacity to be recycled.

Follow-up
Undertake a recycling drive within the school encouraging pupils and staff to put materials like paper and cans in recycling bins rather than in the waste basket. Then repeat the survey and award a prize for the class which has made most progress in recycling and reducing its waste.

National Parks

Age range
Seven to eleven.

Group size
Groups of four.

What you need
Posters, postcards and background information from as many UK National Parks as possible, together with a map showing National Parks; an atlas.

What to do
Explain to the children that they are going to make a study of National Parks in England and Wales. Point out that National Parks were set up to preserve particularly beautiful areas of countryside for future generations to enjoy, and that one of the main aims of the parks is to encourage tourism.

Ask the children to look at a map of National Parks and link this to an atlas map showing the physical geography of the UK. Talk about the types of areas in which National Parks are found, i.e. often mountainous or high areas and sometimes close to the coast. Tell the children to find the nearest large towns and cities, together with the motorways and main roads which link these cities with the National Parks.

Next, divide the class into groups and give each group leaflets, pictures and posters on one National Park. Each group has to produce a report about the park they have studied to include:
- its name and location in the UK;
- its size;
- the types of scenery found there;
- the number of visitors each year;
- the special attractions of the park.

Follow-up
Make a wall display of the National Parks using the work of each group. Add suggestions for possible National Parks in Scotland and Northern Ireland by including maps, pictures and photographs of particularly attractive areas such as the Grampian mountains or the Giant's Causeway.

Antarctica

Age range
Nine to eleven.

Group size
Groups of three or four.

What you need
Maps and photographs of Antarctica including its wildlife, background information on Antarctica from sources such as Friends of the Earth and Greenpeace, reference books on Antarctica.

What to do
Explain to the children the importance to the world of Antarctica. It is the last great wilderness area on earth, but it also has rich reserves of minerals and oil. If possible, arrange for a speaker to visit the school from Greenpeace, Friends of the Earth and a major oil company such as Shell or BP (on separate occasions) to talk about Antarctica. Point out that the main issue is whether the resources of Antarctica be developed or the area be left as wilderness. Linked to this is the question of how far resources can be exploited without damaging the environment. Encourage the children to make notes as they listen to the speakers, to help them form their own opinion later.

Divide the class into groups representing some of the main interests in Antarctica such as large oil companies, national governments (such as UK and Argentina), conservation groups (such as Greenpeace), groups wanting to develop tourism and groups representing the wildlife of Antarctica. Each group should write a short press release saying why they think Antarctica's resources should or should not be developed. A press release should be written on one side only. The first paragraph should sum up the story in about forty words and should be interesting, newsworthy and accurate. The following paragraph(s) should cover any other relevant information or points of interest. A picture or photograph will make the press release more eye-catching. A contact name, address and phone number should also be supplied.

Tell the groups to devise simple posters with pictures and key facts to accompany their press release. Then hold a class debate. The children should elect a president to run the debate and each group should present its case to the class. Afterwards, the other groups can ask questions and raise points for discussion. At the end the children abandon their roles and hold a free vote on whether Antarctica's resources should be developed.

Follow-up
Use a large map of the world with coloured tacks to record places in the news where the environment is under threat, for example through the destruction of wildlife or rain forest or through pollution. The children could also mark on areas where successful projects to save and improve the environment are located.

Links with other curriculum areas

Technology
- designing and making equipment to re-use resources such as paper or textiles.

Mathematics
- number values: quantity and value of resources;
- drawing graphs of different types of pollution, e.g. in parks.

History
- attempts to curtail or stop pollution in the past;
- early attempts at conserving resources;
- setting up public parks in Victorian times.

Natural resources, pollution and conservation

Science
- experimenting on pollution – finding ways to remove it from different substances such as rock and water;
- exploring the properties of resources such as wood, rock, fish.

Art
- junk modelling;
- designing posters to highlight the plight of areas such as Antarctica or the tropical rain forest.

English
- stories and poems about the effect of over-exploitation of resources, e.g.:
- Dust Bowl of the USA in the 1930s
- overfishing in the North Sea;
- destruction of the tropical rainforest area.

Distant places

The study of distant places is one aspect of the Geography National Curriculum which has caused some concern amongst teachers. The crux of the problem is how to make the teaching of life in distant places as real to children as local traffic or local shops. The difficulty is that pupils will probably never have visited the distant locality and so have few points of reference when studying the lives of people in places like West Africa or China. Other difficulties have been the lack of good teaching materials, particularly photographs, slides and artefacts which deal with life in a locality in a distant place. Many reference books deal with entire countries such as Egypt or India but few cover life in a small locality within these countries. This dearth of teaching material is rapidly being overcome by the publication of a series of case study photo-packs produced by groups such as Action Aid, the Geographical Association, Development Education Centres and publishers such as Scholastic (see Resources section for details).

However, problems remain. Most teachers are aware that it would be a mistake to dwell on what is exotic and different about a distant place at the expense of exploring what people around the world have in common.

Similarly, there are pitfalls of over-simplification and stereotyping when dealing with locality studies of distant places. Children who have studied a village in rural India need to be aware that in the same country there are large modern cities with skyscrapers, factories and traffic jams! The purpose of this series of projects is to suggest some ways of approaching the teaching of distant places which will enable the teacher to give a balanced, accurate view of how people live in that place.

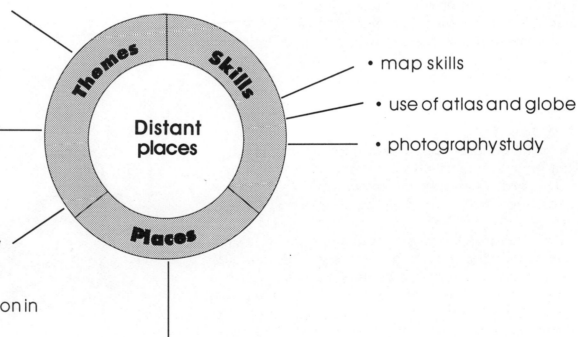

Human geography
• people and their way of life (such as homes, work, education, leisure, journeys) in other parts of the world

Physical geography
• weather in other parts of the world
• plants and animals in other parts of the world

Environmental geography
• resources around the world
• pollution and conservation in other countries

Distant places

Themes

Skills

Places

• map skills
• use of atlas and globe
• photography study

• distant places in other parts of the world

Jobs around the world

Age range
Five to seven.

Group size
Whole class.

What you need
Reference material showing photographs and pictures of people doing different jobs around the world, e.g., a postwoman/man in USA, a firefighter in Australia, a steelworker in Brazil, a farmer in India, a shop worker in Singapore, a train driver in Holland, a shoe cleaner or water seller in Brazil, a person collecting firewood in Mali. Try to obtain pictures showing a range of men and women, countries and formal and informal occupations, such as shop worker and firewood collector; a large world map.

What to do
Explain to the children that they are going to study the different jobs that people do in different parts of the world. This project might well follow logically from one which has been looking at the jobs people do in the local area.

Show the children the photographs and pictures and ask them to talk about what they can see. They should identify on the world map the country each worker is from. In particular, they should focus on what the person (man or woman) is doing, what tools or equipment are involved, if it is indoor or outdoor work and if outdoor, what the weather seems to be like.

Ask each child to choose one worker and, using the reference material, write 'A day in the life of . . .'

account of their chosen worker. This should include as many factual details as possible about that person's life, as well as describing that person's feelings about the job.

Follow-up
Discuss why people do these different jobs all over the world and look for any evidence that men tend to do some jobs and women others.

Select a few of the jobs which may be done in the local area, such as firefighter, nurse, crossing warden, bus driver and talk about similarities and differences between the local example and the corresponding example in the reference material.

Houses around the world

Age range
Five to seven.

Group size
Pairs.

What you need
Photographs of houses in a range of different countries such as Swiss chalets, tall thin Dutch houses, Japanese homes, USA ranch-type houses, tent homes, Dyak long houses, boat houses in the UK and Thailand, Scottish croft, Australian outback or tropical houses; card, paint, brushes, cardboard, adhesive, straw, dowelling and any other suitable model-making material.

What to do
Explain to the children that they are going to be studying different types of houses and homes from countries around the world. Show the whole class some of the photographs and talk about the features of the houses shown such as the need for a steep, overhanging roof in countries like Switzerland which get a lot of rain and snow. Other points to mention include the materials used to build the house, for example, wood, brick, glass, steel, concrete, and features related to local conditions such as flat roofs in hot dry countries on which food can be dried and stored.

Next, let each pair of children choose a photograph then ask them to draw a picture illustrating the home and add a sentence about its shape, structure or building material.

When they have completed their drawing, each pair should make a model of their chosen home using the

materials available. They should try to include as much detail as possible. When complete, the class should combine all their models to make a 'World Village' display each labelled with the flag of its country.

Follow-up
Extend the idea of houses around the world to include models of farm houses and older houses such as castles and forts and add these to the display.

Visitors

Age range
Five to eleven.

Group size
Whole class.

What you need
A person who has spent some time in another country and can talk about it with slides, pictures and artefacts at a level appropriate to the children. Examples of people willing and able to do this include other teachers, parents, governors and even other children in the school (who may be interviewed on tape and the tape used as a stimulus if they are unable or unwilling to talk to a class). Other speakers can be obtained from charities such as Oxfam, Action Aid and Save the Children Fund as well as the Commonwealth Institute in London. If possible, try to get a speaker who has been recommended for giving a good presentation. A world map.

What to do
Explain to the children that they will have a visitor who has spent some time in another country. Make sure that the children locate the country on a large globe and/or a large atlas of the world. Ideally the visit should be timed to coincide with a study the class are already making of a locality in that country, as they would then have some background knowledge about conditions in the area such as weather, relief, roads, villages and towns.

Ask the children to draw up a list of questions to ask the visitor arising from their initial study of the locality,

such as: At what age do children start school? What journeys do people make? Where are the nearest shops? How does the weather change during the year? What are the houses like?

Encourage the children to ask those questions which the visitor has not answered at the end of her talk. They should also ask follow-up questions to aspects of life which came as a surprise to them.

Follow-up
Use the information from the visitor to add to the project on the distant locality.

Using artefacts

Age range
Five to eleven.

Group size
Groups of two, three or four.

What you need
A set of cardboard boxes, one per group, sets of artefacts from another country assembled by you, a colleague, a friend or one of the Development Education Centres to be found around the country. The artefacts of another country may include items such as toys, musical instruments, articles of clothing, bus tickets, printing blocks, cooking utensils and even games.

What to do
Divide the class into groups of three or four and give each group a cardboard box. Explain to them that they have to imagine that in half an hour someone from another country will make a short visit to the class. They will only have time to pick up the cardboard boxes before they have to return to their country. There they will use the contents of the cardboard boxes to teach pupils of a similar age about life in the UK. The task is for each of the groups to fill their cardboard boxes with items which they feel give an accurate impression of their lives. Pupils can collect things from around the classroom and list other items which they might bring from home if more time were available.

At the end of half an hour each group should share the contents of their box with the rest of the class. They should talk about why they selected the items they did. discuss with the rest of the class what impression people in another country would get of life in the UK from each box. The aims of this activity are to show that a lot can be learned from ordinary, everyday objects and to make children aware of jumping to false conclusions and resorting to over-simplification.

Next, move to a study of a set of objects from another country. Display the objects on a table and ask the children in pairs to choose one object to study that interests them. The key questions for the children to consider about the objects are:
- Where does it come from?
- What is it made of?
- What is it used for?
- Is it old or new?
- Was it made by machine or by hand?
- Was it bought?

Ask the children to think about other questions they would like answered about the object, such as who made it or who used it. Then ask each pair to show their object and to say what they have been able to find out about it from background information, pictures and photographs of the country, as well as information from the teacher or visitors. They should emphasise what the objects show about life in the other country.

Photographs of distant places

Age range
Five to eleven.

Group size
Pairs or groups of four.

What you need
A set of photographs of the area around the school, which can be taken by the children or by the teacher or together. A set of photographs of a distant locality, e.g., Chambakole, Pampagrande (from Action Aid, see Resources section), St Lucia (Geographical Association), A3 sheets of paper, pens.

What to do
Photographs are an important and popular resource for teaching about distant places. They focus the children's attention, stimulate talk and can be used to introduce wider experiences. Explain that the children will be looking at sets of photographs starting with some of the local area.

Display the photographs of the local area and get the children to work in pairs to select from them six or eight to send a class of similar age children in another country to show what life is like in this part of the UK. Once each pair has made their selection, encourage them to discuss their choices with other pairs. Which photographs do they all choose? Which ones does no-one choose? Discuss with the children the idea that sets of photographs can be selected to convey a particular image of a place. For example, ask them to choose six photographs which show the most positive side of the local area. Then let them choose six photographs which give a more negative impression. The purpose is for children to realise that the photographs of distant places they have seen have been selected by someone and may not tell the whole story of life in that place, and so should be viewed with careful consideration. This may also help children begin to acknowledge the stereotyped way in which Western nations perceive 'third world' countries.

Next, display the photographs of the distant place. In pairs, the children should choose one photograph that interests them. They should then put it in the centre of an A3 sheet of paper and annotate it with as many questions about the photograph as they can think of. For example: What are the people in the photograph doing? What is the weather like? What are the plants shown? Where was the machine built? and so on. The aim of the activity is to encourage children to look in detail at a photograph, and so focus on foreground, background, left side, right side and so on, rather than just glance at the photograph and gain a sketchy impression.

The children should then write speech or thought bubbles for the characters in the photographs. Each pair can then write a series of captions for their photograph and read these to the rest of the class in an attempt to select the most appropriate.

Visits to other places

Age range
Seven to eleven.

Group size
Whole class.

What you need
Paint, brushes, paper.

What to do
Talk to the children about the places they have visited either on holidays or on visits to friends and relatives. Some visits will be to quite local places, others to places in the UK and some to places in other countries.

Ask the children to describe one place they visited and to draw a picture of its main features. Then ask them to think about some of the events they witnessed/experienced during their trip, for example, festivals or celebrations, boat trips, mountain walks, visits to castles and so on. Then ask them to incorporate a chosen event into a cartoon strip story. Explain that it needs to be a story that can be depicted in 6 pictures (frames) to make up the strip. The story should involve the people and features of that distant place, and can show dialogue or have an explanatory line beneath each frame. The aim is to develop narrative and sequencing within the context of a different place.

Twinning

Age range
Nine to eleven.

Group size
Groups of three or four.

What you need
Maps, brochures, pictures of the twin town.

What to do
Find out from the local council the name of the town or village abroad with which your local town or village is twinned. Many British towns have twinning arrangements with towns in France, Germany and the Netherlands and others even further afield. If possible, set up links with a school in the twin town and arrange to borrow a set of maps, brochures and photographs which show what life is like for people there.

If possible, find a local person who has visited the twin town and is willing to come and talk about what it is like. Ask the children to write letters about themselves and their lives and homes to children of a similar age at the link school in the twin town. Use the information from this to develop a series of project folders about life in the twin town under such headings as: food, houses, transport, buildings, leisure, shops and shopping, jobs and landscape. The children should pool their information so that each group can produce a folder on one theme which they present to the rest of the class.

Follow-up
Make a video of the class, their school and the local area and send this to the twin school to encourage them to do the same for their area.

Links with other curriculum areas

Technology
- designing and making promotional videos for exotic and non-exotic distant places.

Art and music
- different types of art and music in different parts of the world, e.g.,
– Polynesian art and music;
– Inuit art;
– Native American art and music.

Mathematics
- estimation and measurement in relation to maps and distances.
- sorting in relation to images, jobs, places.

Distant places

Science
- weather in different parts of the world – the causes of variations in temperature and rainfall from place to place.

History
- growth of empires and spread of nations outwards.
- impact of colonial era on countries around the world.

English
- stories and poems about adventures to distant places, including journeys, voyages, visits, trips.

Reproducibles

UK map

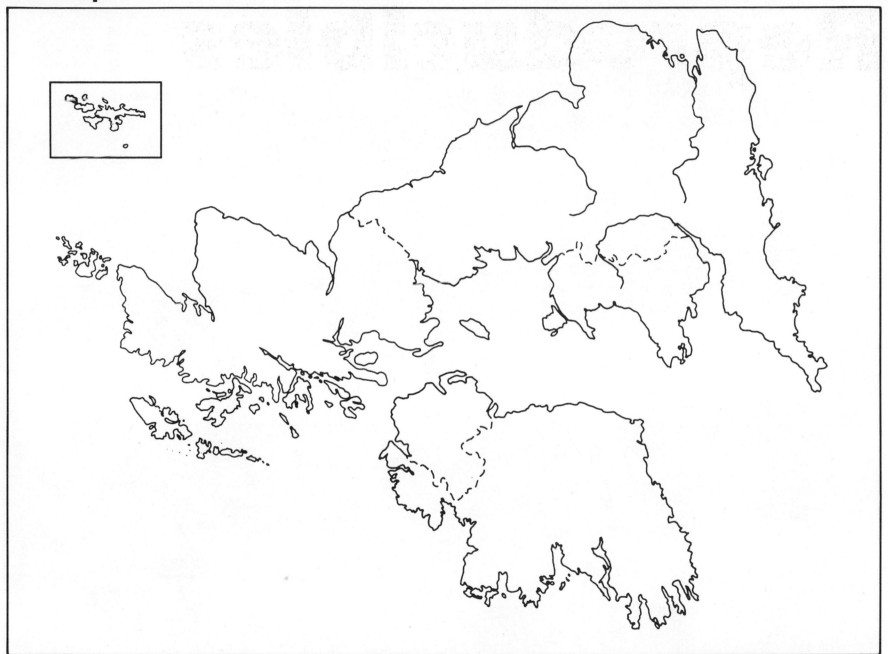

World map

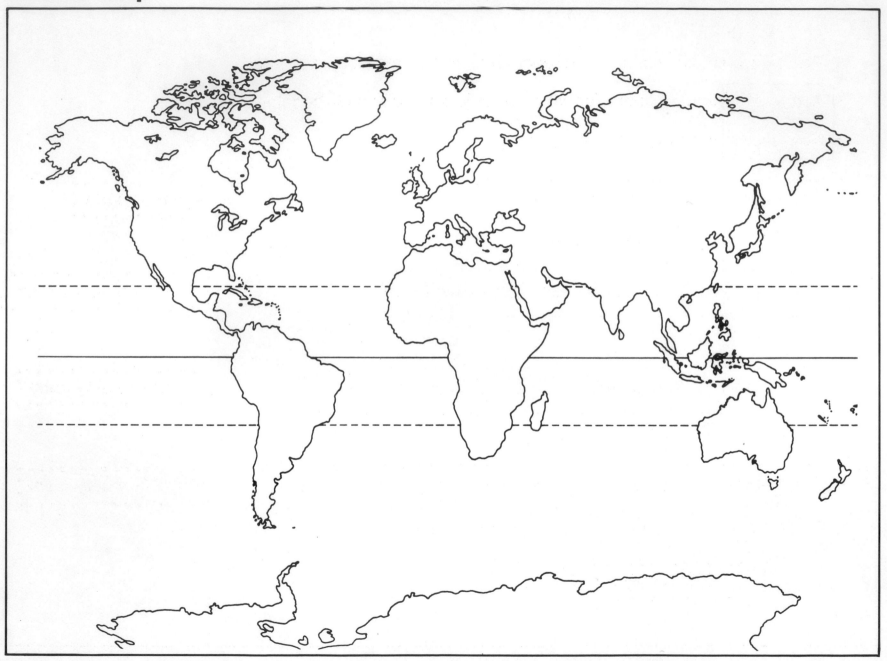

The dirty hands soil test, see page 13

- First take a small amount of soil, enough to fill the palm of a small hand.

- Add a small amount (a few drops) of water to the soil and mix together.

- Now answer the following questions.

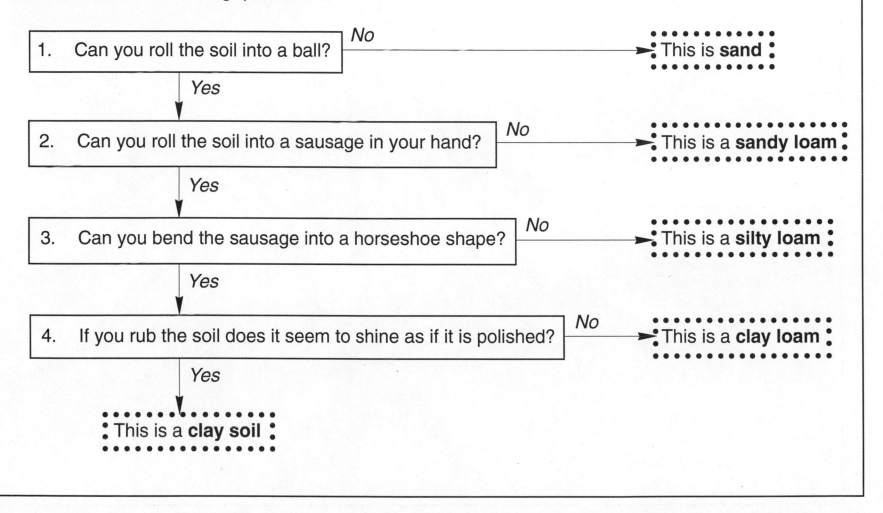

1. Can you roll the soil into a ball? — *No* → This is **sand**

    Yes ↓

2. Can you roll the soil into a sausage in your hand? — *No* → This is a **sandy loam**

    Yes ↓

3. Can you bend the sausage into a horseshoe shape? — *No* → This is a **silty loam**

    Yes ↓

4. If you rub the soil does it seem to shine as if it is polished? — *No* → This is a **clay loam**

    Yes ↓

This is a **clay soil**

Make a volcano, see page 25

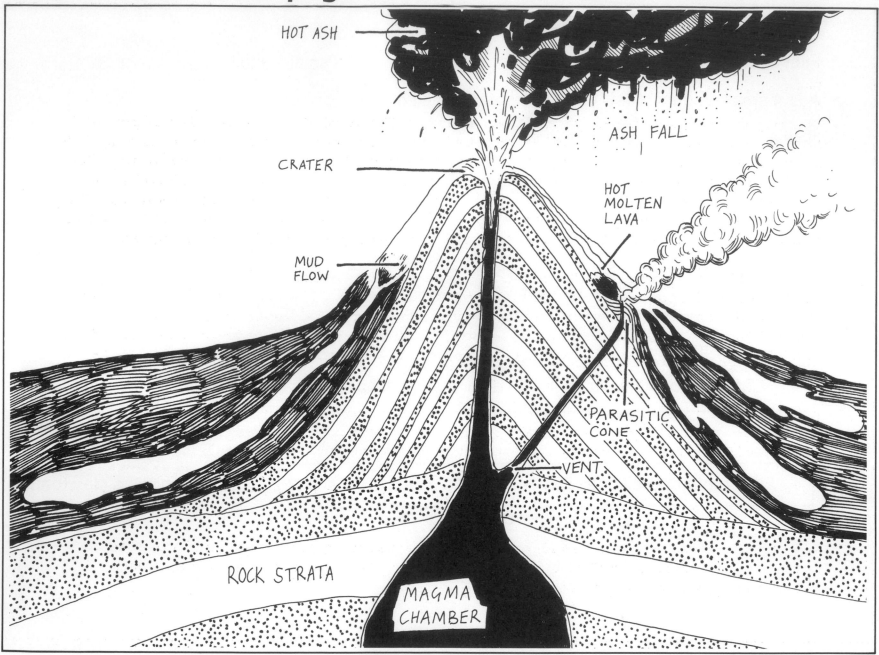

HOT ASH

ASH FALL

CRATER

HOT MOLTEN LAVA

MUD FLOW

PARASITIC CONE

VENT

ROCK STRATA

MAGMA CHAMBER

Mount St Helens, see page 29

Telex: 18 May 1980

The major eruption began at 8.32 am Pacific Standard Time. A massive blast of hot gases, ash, rock and ice devastated the surrounding area. People living 150 kilometres away were thrown out of their beds by the force of the eruption. An earthquake accompanied the eruption. This shook loose a massive avalanche of mud, water, rock and ice. Some of the avalanche slammed into nearby Spirit Lake. The water level in the lake rose 70 metres and water surged 130 metres up the surrounding land, felling trees and smothering the land in mud and ash.

Some of the avalanche followed the course of the Toutle River. It filled the valley with deposits of mud and ash to a depth of 200 metres. A wall of water, mud and ash flowed down the valley at 20 kilometres per hour destroying everything in its path. Roads and bridges were washed away and houses buried to roof level. Large numbers of elk, deer, squirrel, rabbits and other wildlife were killed.

All trees for 11 kilometres around the volcano were flattened like matchwood. Clouds of ash fell on towns like Yakima 80 kilometres eastwards. The dense ash turned midday into darkness and streetlights came on automatically.

Fifty-seven people are reported dead or missing, including some local people who refused to leave their homes.

420 square kilometres of land has been devastated by the blast and covered in hot volcanic debris. 500 metres of the volcano's summit has just vanished - blown away as ash and avalanches.

Earthquake – Mexico City

At 7.20 am on Thursday 19 September 1985 the world's largest city was struck by an earthquake. Pavements buckled, the earth cracked open, buildings collapsed and thousands died.

At 7.38 pm on Saturday 21 September 1985 a second earthquake struck the city. Thirty thousand people died in the two earthquakes. Over 900 blocks of flats and offices collapsed. Half the hospital wards and 500 schools in the city were wrecked. Electricity and telephone lines were broken and water and sewage pipes were burst open.

The Central Hospital, a 12-storey building, was reduced to a pile of rubble only four storeys high; hundreds of patients and medical staff were trapped inside. Gas pipes fractured and the gas caught light, setting fire to buildings nearby. People were trapped in lifts in tall blocks of flats, offices and hotels. Hundreds of people were trapped in the ruins of collapsed flats, hotels and hospitals. Teams of rescue workers tried to move the concrete with their bare hands when they heard the cries of trapped children. The underground railway came to a halt with trains trapped in tunnels with no light or power as people struggled to escape from the underground.

Compass directions, see page 65

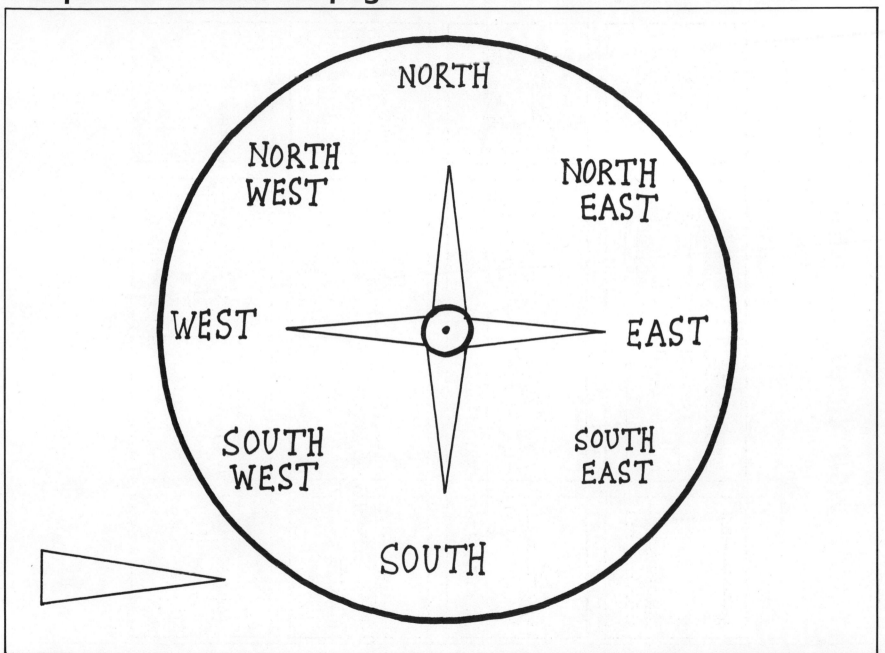

Farm visit questionnaire

Name of farm	Size of farm
Location	
Crops grown	Animals reared
Buildings (number and uses)	Machinery
Types of field boundary (hedges/fences/walls)	Soil types
Main sources of income	Number of workers
Other questions I would like to ask	

Plan views, see page 64

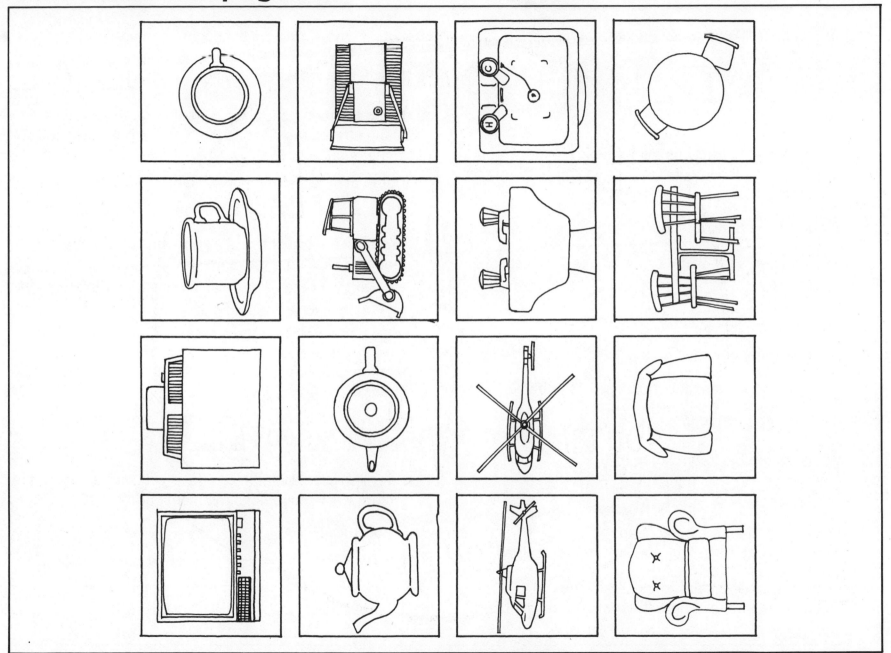

Stream study, see page 58

Name..Date.............................

Tick your position: 1 ☐   2 ☐   3 ☐   4 ☐

Weather...

Follow the same instructions for each part of the stream you study. Don't rush into the water – LOOK – Try not to disturb too much.

1. Stand on the bank and look.

2. What colour is the water?

    clear ☐   murky ☐

    Why do you think it is that colour?

3. What colour is the mud on the bottom of the stream?

4. How would you describe the slope of the banks?

    steep ☐   gentle ☐

5. What are the banks made up of?

    sand ☐   pebbles ☐   soil ☐   clay ☐

6. Does the soil on the bank change?
    How? Look at the colour and size of the pebbles.

7. How deep do the plant roots grow? Look at the sides of the stream where the roots will be exposed.

8. Look at the stream. Is it straight or curved?

9. How fast is the water flowing?   slowly ☐   rapidly ☐

10. Using the metre stick, measure the depth at each side of the stream (as close to the bank as possible) and in the middle.

    Depth at side   Depth in middle   Depth at side

    ....cm   ....cm   ....cm

11. (a) Go to the top of the bank and measure along it 2 metres, following the stream flow.

    (b) Mark your start and finishing position with 2 pencils.

    (c) Go back to your start position.

    (d) Put the orange in the stream and at the same time start the stop-watch. As the orange reaches the 2 metre mark turn off the stop-watch. Do this for each side of the stream.

    How many seconds did the orange take to travel 2m?

    camp side ....   far side ....

12. Be a detective. What things have you noticed about the stream which have not been mentioned?

    (a)...

    (b)...

    (c)...

    (d)...

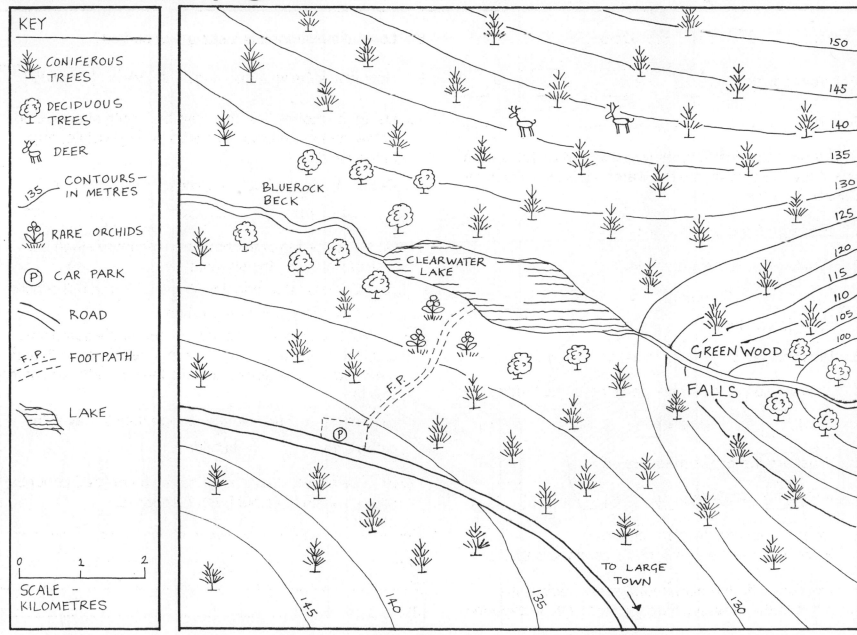

KEY

	CONIFEROUS TREES
	DECIDUOUS TREES
	DEER
135	CONTOURS— IN METRES
	RARE ORCHIDS
P	CAR PARK
	ROAD
F.P.	FOOTPATH
	LAKE

0   1   2
SCALE – KILOMETRES

BLUEROCK BECK

CLEARWATER LAKE

F.P.

150
145
140
135
130
125
120
115
110
105
100

GREENWOOD FALLS

TO LARGE TOWN

145
140
135
130

Using water, see page 52

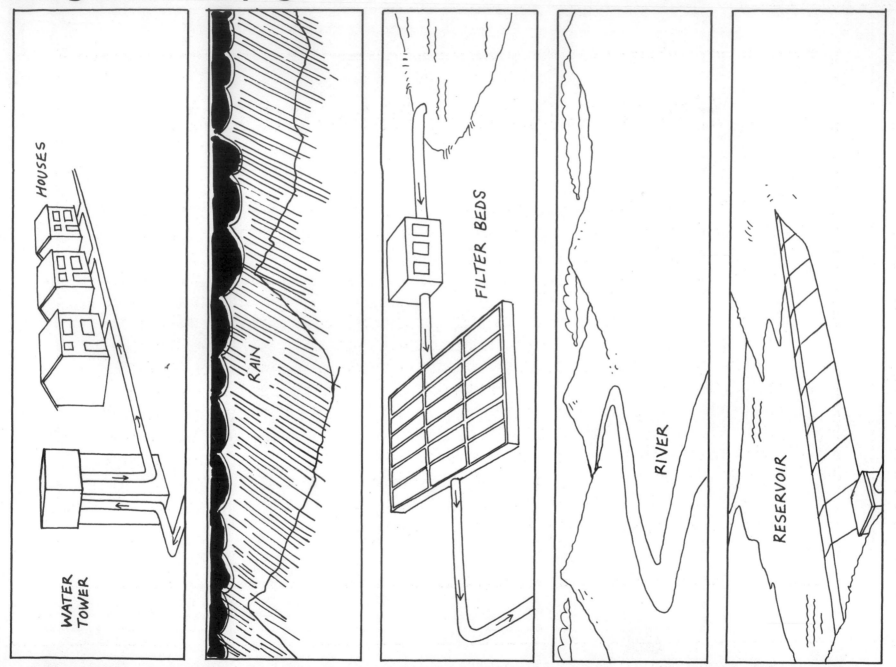

HOUSES

WATER TOWER

RAIN

FILTER BEDS

RIVER

RESERVOIR